POWER INTERVIEWS

POWER INTERVIEWS

Job-Winning Tactics from Fortune 500 Recruiters

Revised and Expanded

Neil Yeager
Lee Hough

John Wiley & Sons, Inc.
New York • Chichester • Weinheim • Brisbane • Singapore • Toronto

Copyright © 1990, 1998 by Neil Yeager and Lee Hough
Published by John Wiley & Sons, Inc.

Library of Congress Cataloging-in-Publication Data

Yeager, Neil M.
    Power interviews : job winning tactics from Fortune 500 recruiters
/ Neil Yeager, Lee Hough. — Rev. and expanded ed.
      p.   cm
    Includes index.
    ISBN 0-471-17788-1 (paper)
    1. Employment interviewing.   I. Hough, Lee.   II. Title.
HF5549.5.I6Y43   1998
650.14—dc21   97-35196
                                                CIP

11

To Cletha and Ben who are always there for me.
—Neil Yeager

To Carol, you are the best.
—Lee Hough

Contents

Preface to the Revised Edition

Since the first edition of this book was published in 1990, the workplace has become increasingly different from the workplace most of us were used to.

Lifetime employment in a predictable, slow-moving, multilayered, bureaucratic organization has almost ceased to exist. The Old Compact of good work in exchange for job security has been replaced by the new reality—that all employment is in fact temporary employment, what some people refer to as "You Incorporated."

The New Compact requires new rules and new skills, one of which is the power interview. The power interview has become necessary, since you are likely to be competing for jobs with others who are equally or better qualified for the job you are trying to get. What will differentiate you from the competition and eventually enable you to prevail is your capacity to perform better in the interview.

If you doubt that the competition is getting steeper, consider that, in addition to competing with new graduates, whose information technology skills may well be more state-of-the-art than yours, a critical new mass of competition is the group of qualified people who have lost their jobs as the result of layoffs. For example, if you are looking for work in telecommunications, your competition will include the 40,000 AT&T workers laid off in 1995–96; if you're looking for work in high-tech industries, you will be competing with the 83,000 laid off at IBM and Digital; in retail you'll be competing with the 50,000 let go at Sears. The last few years have seen a tremendous flooding of the job market as a result of downsizing, and all indications are the trend will continue into the 21st century.

What this means is that you had better be better at selling yourself than the competition or you will not win the job. *Power Interviews* will give you the information and skills you need to compete in this increasingly competitive marketplace. You will learn what to say and how to say it and what not to say. You will learn about the New Compact that defines the emerging changing relationship between employer and employee. You will learn about the trends affecting the companies you are trying to join and how to show them that you understand the impact of these trends on their success. You will learn how to read between the lines when conducting the interview so that you can differentiate yourself from the competition. And finally, to make sure that your power interviews ultimately result in getting the job you really want, you will learn how to consider carefully whether to accept an offer once you have one.

—Neil Yeager
Amherst, Massachusetts

—Lee Hough
Scottsdale, Arizona

Introduction

Whether you've been in the job market for a long time or are just entering it, you probably know that career mobility is the model for the 21st century. People change jobs, organizations, and even professions more frequently than ever before. Although this increased mobility creates potential problems, it also offers great opportunities. To take advantage of the best opportunities, those seeking them must become adept at job interviewing. The need to become highly proficient in the interview process is highlighted by the fact that you will most likely engage in the process more frequently than you might expect or wish, and will face increased competition. The trend of mergers, buyouts, and acquisitions—a trend that most experts contend will continue into the 21st century—leaves even those who feel most secure exposed to the possibility of finding themselves suddenly in the job market. Continued efforts at reorganization, even within companies that remain intact, increase the likelihood that you may no longer be needed or that you won't like the plans your organization creates for you.

Your ability to create a successful interview and win over your interviewer will determine the extent to which you will find the career marketplace full of opportunities or full of disappointment. Regardless of your qualifications for a position, if you cannot give a winning performance in the interview, you will probably not get the job. Like any other discipline or area of expertise, interviewing is a skill, which if studied and practiced can become an important part of your repertoire of competencies.

This book will teach you to master the art and science of interviewing. You will be taught the inside secrets of interviewing in the corporate world. You will be briefed on the key trends for the 21st century, trends that are on the minds of every corporate leader and every interviewer in the United States. You will develop strategies for reading your interviewer so that you present yourself in a way that makes the most powerful impact. You will discover what not to do in an interview by learning from the mistakes others have made. You will find out what those in the corporate world who do the hiring are most concerned about and how to address those concerns. You will learn how and when to negotiate the best offer possible. Finally, you will learn strategies for determining whether you should take a particular job once you receive an offer.

At the end of each chapter you will find a self-test called the Power Prep Strategy. Each Power Prep Strategy is designed to help you get the most out of that chapter and to fine-tune your skill and knowledge base in that aspect of power interviewing.

Practice and follow the advice presented in this book and you will get far more offers than you need. Refine your interviewing skill to the point where it becomes one of your strongest areas and you will find yourself with an unlimited range of offers from which to choose.

The information presented in this book is based on many years of experience on both sides of the marketplace. To avoid cumbersome language we use the pronouns *we* and *I* as appropriate. In general, "I" statements having to do with clients seeking work refer to Neil Yeager, and "I" statements having to do with recruiting refer to Lee Hough.

1

The Basics of Power Interviewing

Preparation is the foundation of power interviewing. There are many ways to prepare for an interview and many areas in which to prepare. The more prepared you are, the more powerful your impact in an interview will be. While much of the basic advice is common sense, it seems that many people, caught in the intensity of the job search, miss some of the fine points. What follows is a reminder of what to do and not to do to keep from shooting yourself in the foot.

INTERVIEWING BASICS

Be Real

Although an interview is a performance, people sometimes think that they should put on an act. Interviewers, faced with increased turnover, are becoming more skilled at interviewing. Most can spot a phony applicant very quickly. Being sincere and forthright, while at the same time targeting your presentation to the needs of the interviewer, is the best approach. If your acting is good enough to fool a knowledgeable interviewer, you should be on stage or in the movies. Most people are much more successful if they present an honest view of themselves that matches who they really are.

Be Together

Being together means paying attention to things you usually take for granted. Timeliness, knowing where you're going, food, rest, and dress are all part of being together. Careful attention to these details is worth your consideration, because people are often judged by such factors. It makes sense to have your act together in these areas so that you aren't eliminated before you have a chance to state your case.

Be On Time

In a world where time is of the essence (in most successful companies), lateness is tantamount to heresy. It is the kiss of death in an interview. When you're late for an interview, even with a good excuse (some say there's no such thing), you immediately place yourself at the bottom of the heap. It's important to remember that the interview process actually begins before the interview. It begins when either party decides to pursue an interview. You will be judged on your behavior as soon as the process begins, not just during the actual interview.

Know Where You Are Going

If you've ever been late for an important appointment, you know how stressful that can be. If you've ever been kept waiting for an important appointment, you know how annoying that can be. If you don't know where you are going, your anxiety about getting there will be high. The best thing to do is to travel the route of your destination before the day of the interview. If that's not possible, at least give yourself plenty of time to get to where you're going in case you get lost.

Get Food and Rest

It's difficult to perform well if you're tired and hungry. Although the anxiety brought on by a high-stakes interview can cause you to lose your appetite or a night's sleep, make every effort to be rested and fed before the meeting. There are enough things to focus on in the interview besides your body's need for food and rest.

Dress Properly

So much has been written about dressing for success that we need not elaborate here. What's important to remember is that you will be judged by your appearance. Know that in most successful companies people are expected to look the part. The interviewer will assume that you will look your best in the interview. If your best is not up to par with their standards, you will have a difficult time convincing them that you are an eligible applicant. If you're unsure of a particular organization's dress code (they all have one), there's a simple way to find out. A few days before your interview, position yourself at the front of the building where your interview is going to take place and observe what the employees entering the building are wearing. Choose the best-dressed people you see and model your interview clothes after theirs. Organizations are concerned with finding people who fit in, and this is one way of showing that you would be a good match.

If this approach is impractical for you, pick up one of the more conservative business-related magazines, see what people in them are wearing, and use that as a model. Another approach, if you've got the budget, is to go to an upscale clothing store, find responsive salespersons, tell them what your needs are, and let them go to work: it's what they do for a living.

THE INSIDE SECRETS OF INTERVIEWING

In addition to the basic preparation just discussed, you can do several things throughout the interview process that will save you time and energy and ensure that you are tapping your opportunities to the fullest extent. Keep these ten points in mind and rely on them for managing the interview process.

1. Avoid Human Resources

In most organizations the human resource department is the obvious place to go if you're looking for a job. The problem is that in most organizations the people in human resources are the least powerful when it comes to offering jobs (unless you're looking for a job in personnel). Usually the job of this department is to screen applicants, keeping those they deem inappropriate from the real decision makers. Your best bet is to try to talk with the people in the department in which you want to work. If you find that you must navigate your way through human resources to get to your target, remember that the people there are generally "gatekeepers" in the hiring process, and your task is to convince them to let you through the gate.

2. Don't Rely on Ads

Because the most obvious source of job openings is a newspaper's classified ad section, many people mistakenly assume that it is the richest. The fact is, many jobs never appear in the papers, and most jobs don't get filled as the result of newspaper ads. We know of one marketing manager for a large computer firm who in 15 years had hired over two thousand marketing representatives yet had never placed an ad in the newspaper. Imagine the poor soul searching for a job as a marketing rep in that company and waiting for the ad to appear in the paper.

3. Specify Your Job Requirements

The worst thing you can do in presenting yourself to a prospective employer is to suggest that you're a generalist, capable of doing a broad range of jobs. Although you want eventually to convey the fact that you have a range of skills to offer, you should begin by presenting your specialty. Failure to indicate a specific set of skills, those that are your strongest, implies that you're not really good at anything. The more specific you can be in identifying the kind of work you want, the better. If you can do some research ahead of time to determine what areas are in demand in that company and can target one of those as your specialty, you'll have a great edge over the competition.

4. Have a Professionally Printed Résumé

This may seem obvious to you, but it is amazing how many people think that the way their paperwork looks is relatively unimportant. Keep in mind that your résumé is often the first thing someone sees that has anything to do with you. These days, when even junk mail has a high-quality look, it's important to make sure that your paperwork is top-notch. Most interviewers make the assumption that the quality of your résumé is a reflection of the quality of the work you do. If it's not top quality, you're not a top candidate.

5. Tell Everyone You're in the Market

If you're just getting out of school, you want to tell everyone you know that you're looking for work. The more specific you can be about the kind of work you want, the better. Saying "I want a job in the accounting department of a large corporation" is much better than saying "I need a job." Since you don't yet have a network of past employers and colleagues, you need to tap the network you do have. Sources for referrals and contacts include family, church members, other recent graduates, fraternities, sororities, service clubs, professors, insurance agents, brokers, and any other people you or your family have done business with. If you've already been in the workforce, you can use all these sources plus any others you've generated in the course of your working life. Some people have a problem with the idea of broadcasting their need or desire for new work. Those dissatisfied with their jobs often feel that they should keep their dissatisfaction a secret to avoid problems or awkwardness at their current job. Unfortunately this strategy is a great drawback to getting and winning interviews. If people who have the power to hire don't know you're looking, chances are slim that they will approach you for an interview. You need to broadcast your desires as often and as widely as possible to ensure that you get the opportunity to sell yourself to desirable buyers. This may create temporary discomfort while you're still on the job and in transition, but it will ultimately lead to many more, and much better, offers.

6. Conduct Prospecting Interviews

Sitting around waiting for a response to your letters and résumés is like staying at home, watching TV, and waiting to meet "the right person." It simply won't happen. To increase the likelihood of getting job interviews, you must get out there and interview people in your preferred area to find out what their needs are and to let them know you are available. You may or may not get job offers from doing this, but you will probably get offers for job interviews, which will ultimately lead to job offers.

A good idea before approaching someone in your field of interest, or an organization you want to work in, is to do some research on that field or company. Here's one approach that seems to work well for many people.

Contact the local branch of a national brokerage firm and ask to speak to a broker. Chances are you'll be given someone who is trying to build a clientele and is eager to help you. Tell this person you are not interested in investing at the moment but would like to start a professional relationship with an investment broker. If the broker agrees to work with you (most will), ask for any research materials the firm has on your particular area of interest or industry. The broker can get you general and specific research on a breakdown of all major firms in your industry; opinion on the industry, both short- and long-term; and information on a specific company that will include financial data, business developments, and positive and negative events affecting the company. You will also get names, addresses, and telephone numbers that will enable you to contact companies.

Once you have this information, approach people in the industries or organizations you're interested in. Tell them you want 15 minutes of their time to talk with them about prospects in their field. Most people will give you the 15 minutes and more. Ask them what they like about what they do, what they don't like about it, how they got started, and what they would do to break into the field today. Be careful not to take more than the 15 minutes you asked for. At the end of that time, tell them you're enjoying talking with them but that you don't want to take any more of their time than agreed upon. They will greatly appreciate this consideration, may even give you more time, and will feel they've been dealing with a person who respects them.

The result of this effort will be contacts, leads, interviews, and perhaps even job offers.

7. Follow Up

The people who get the important interviews, and the important jobs, are the ones who understand the importance of follow-up. If you're talking to the right people, they are most likely very busy people. Chances are, unless you are someone they really need at the moment, they are not going to keep you in the forefront of their minds. One thing you can do to ensure that they remember who you are when they do need someone like you is to be thorough in your follow-up activity. This means sending thank-you letters to everyone you speak with; making follow-up phone calls periodically to see if their needs have changed; and maintaining open lines of communication with them, either through the mail or, if possible, through mutual network connections. When considering whether follow-up is important, think of the following reasons for doing it:

- It informs the company that you are serious about the position.
- Nine out of ten candidates don't follow up.
- It shows you are a thorough person.
- If you are not hired and the position becomes available once again, your name will be fresh in their minds.
- It allows you another opportunity to include information you may have forgotten in the interview.
- It gives you the opportunity to reiterate any crucial points.

8. Monitor Your Activities

If you're conducting a thorough job search, you're very busy. Don't rely on your memory for keeping you on your toes. If you're doing a good job seeking work, you'll probably be on an emotional roller coaster of hope and disappointment from close calls. Your focus on the near miss is important, but once that episode is over it's important to regroup and focus on other prospects. If you've got a good system for monitoring your activities, you won't be left high and dry when your dream job falls through. Keep a close record of all your activities throughout your job search and you'll be assured of an endless supply of tasks to perform that will help you ultimately to achieve your goal.

9. Ask a Friend for Help

The job search can be terribly lonely and frustrating. A good friend with a good ear and, most important, a clear perspective, can help you stay focused, motivated, and organized. While in the throes of job seeking, it is quite easy to become demoralized. Having someone to debrief you after bungled interviews (they happen to everyone) can save you much time and wasted energy brooding over what you should have done. Having someone who is invested in helping you make it through the process, and not necessarily invested in the outcome, is what you want. Your spouse or current interest can be supportive but is probably too closely involved to be of real concrete help. You want someone around who's good at getting you back on track and helping you stay there.

10. Practice Interviewing

You will, we hope, never get so experienced at interviewing that you become an expert. If you're like most people, interviewing is something that you hope to do as infrequently as possible. Ideally you will find a job and an organization to satisfy your needs for an extended period of time. However, be assured that unless you are about to retire (and even then), the odds are you are not done interviewing. Interviewing may be required infrequently, but it is unrealistic to think that you can just do it, and perform well on command. You need to practice. You can practice by yourself in the mirror, with a friend, while driving in your car, or in your idle moments. The important thing is to focus on the aspects of interviewing that make you uncomfortable and work on them until they feel less threatening. One good strategy before an interview is to think of the questions that might be asked that make you the most nervous. Write them down and have someone ask you them. Keep practicing until you've formulated the best responses to each of the difficult questions. You will enter the interview far more prepared, and far less anxious. The results will be far more powerful.

UNDERSTANDING THE NEW COMPACT

Perhaps the most fundamental shift in the career marketplace—one that could very well place you in the ranks of those needing to power interview—is the New Compact. The New Compact reflects a shift in the corporate employment model from long-term stable employment to permanent temporary employment. All jobs are now, by virtue of the New Compact, temporary. What exactly is the New Compact? It is an implicit—although increasingly explicit—agreement on the way things are in the emergent corporation of the 21st century. To understand the New Compact better, it is helpful to examine eight shifts that comprise the essence of that emergent contract between employer and employee. Each of these shifts has implications for how you work and how you power interview for the best jobs.

Shift 1: From Employment for Life to Mutual Benefit Employment

One of the basic tenets of the New Compact is that the expectations of job longevity have changed. No longer can you expect to stay put in one job, or within one organization, for life. Anyone who has been in the marketplace in the last few years knows that employers expect employees to regularly move within organizations, adding value wherever and however they can, and eventually move on when their added value is no longer evident. Mutual benefit employment suggests that the individual and organization will have an arrangement that meets the needs of both parties. Once either party ceases to see the benefit in the relationship, that relationship will cease to exist.

Power Interviewing Implications

What this shift means for the power interview is that as the interviewee and potential hire, you had better be able to articulate in no uncertain terms how you can add value for your prospective organization. In The New Compact your work history counts much less than your potential contribution to meeting your prospective employer's current and immediately anticipated needs. Know what those needs are and speak to them or your interview will quickly stall.

Shift 2: From Bureaucracy to Learning Organization

When bureaucracy was (not long ago) the primary form for most major corporations, the task of the job applicant was to make a case for why he or she should be chosen to play a part in perpetuating that bureaucracy. However, bureaucracies are quickly becoming dinosaurs and anyone keeping a hand on the pulse of the contemporary corporation knows that any company clinging to bureaucratic ways will soon be extinct. As organizations give up the comfort and predictability of the bureaucratic model, the notion that is replacing it most vigorously in many companies is the concept of the learning organization. The term *learning organization* was coined by Peter Senge of MIT in his groundbreaking book *The Fifth Discipline: The Art and Practice of the Learning Organization* (Doubleday/Currency 1990). It has become increasingly common to find proponents of the learning organization in large corporations. The term and the concept suggest that organizations that work to maintain their competitiveness need to subscribe to certain principles, or what Senge calls "disciplines." They are: Personal Mastery, Mental Models, Shared Vision, Team Learning, and Systems Thinking.

Since the learning organization is rapidly becoming the organizational model of choice for many future-oriented organizations, it would be wise for you at least to be familiar with the concept and at best to weave an understanding of the disciplines of a learning organization into the interview.

The Five Disciplines of Learning Organizations

Here is a brief tutorial on the key elements of learning organizations, as defined by Senge.

Personal Mastery Personal mastery involves continually clarifying and deepening your personal vision and commiting yourself to the realization of that vision through the development of your talents. Ideally it involves creating an individual vision that is in alignment with the organization's vision. This alignment fosters the individual reaching his or her potential while meeting the goals of the organization.

Mental Models Mental models involve the discipline of understanding one's personal view of the world and how that filter influences one's view. Our mental models reflect our assumptions, generalizations, and perspectives on our environment. Working with mental models involves turning the mirror inward to better understand what we see and experience. Learning organizations create shared mental models that enable people to understand and work with each other more effectively.

Shared Vision Shared vision involves building a sense of mutual commitment to a set of values, goals, and ideals for an organization. When there is a truly shared vision present among organizational members, there exists a sense of genuine commitment and enrollment to the goals of the organization far beyond that of the mere compliance of people who are simply aligned around the vision of a leader.

Team Learning Team learning involves creating conditions that promote the potential effectiveness of a team beyond that of its individual members. When team learning is present, members are engaging in dialogue that results in their thinking together. The capacity for solving problems together is far greater than the capacity of any individual.

Systems Thinking Systems thinking involves a way of looking at organizations that recognizes the impact of every aspect of an organization on every other aspect. By focusing on the interrelatedness of each aspect of an organization, this approach helps us to better understand change in organizations and the impact that any change can have on other organizational aspects.

Power Interviewing Implications

Here are the implications of these trends for the power interview:

Personal Mastery Organizations are increasingly handing responsibility for career development over to their employees, giving up the paternalistic role they traditionally played (more on this later). They expect employees to take responsibility for continuously developing and honing the skills and talents that make them valued employees. The assumption behind personal mastery is that you have the motivation and ability to identify and build the skill set that the company needs from you. Taking a proactive stance on your professional development and demonstrating that you are a self-starter in the management of your career will gain you signficant points in the power interview.

Mental Models To be effective in the power interview it would be wise to understand the mental models that pervade the organization you are approaching. Mental models often reflect the culture of the organization—and demonstrating an understanding of an organization's culture is often a key to a successful power interview. Before the interview do the best you can to gain an understanding of the organization's prevalent mental models. Is it an organization obsessed with quality— one that places an emphasis on generating and acting on fact-based information? Is it numbers-driven, with a primary emphasis on the bottom line? Is it team-based, always focused on dismantling stovepipes and building cross-functional relationships?

The point here is that every company has its dominant points of focus that help define the organization. Understanding what these focal points are and how they influence the ways in which the people in the organization think will serve you well in the power interview.

Shared Vision Vision is "in." Organizational leaders, having realized that if they don't have a clear understanding of where they are trying to take their organization they are unlikely to get there, are spending an enormous amount of time, money, and energy gaining clarity on their corporate vision. The expectation in the learning organization is that employees are spending an equal amount of time formulating their own visions for their own careers and working on carefully aligning those personal visions with those of the organization. The savvy applicant would be wise to do his or her homework. Gain an understanding of the company's vision (make sure your information is up to date) and think about ways to convey the linkages you see between your personal vision for your own career and the vision of the organization.

Team Learning Team learning is so ubiquitous that any applicant not prepared to talk about his or her experience with teams is vulnerable and likely to end up in the discard pile. Whether or not you have been part of an organization that has operated with formal teams, you need to realize that teams are everywhere. Be prepared to talk about your teamwork skills and your understanding of the value that teamwork has to offer, or be prepared for rejection.

Systems Thinking While systems thinking and its complexity (as defined by Peter Senge and his colleagues at MIT) can be a bit overwhelming, what's important here is to realize the impact that the big picture has on the inner workings of an organization. Most simply put, systems thinking reflects the ripple-in-the-pond effect, the notion that anything of significance that happens in any part of an organization has an impact on all the other parts of the organization similar to the effect observed when one drops a stone in a pond and witnesses the ripple that the stone creates in the rest of the pond. You don't have to become an expert on systems thinking to do well in an interview, unless systems thinking is one of the prevalent mental models in the organization you are approaching, but it would serve you well to demonstrate an understanding of the complexities of organizational life via an understanding of systems thinking.

Shift 3: From Hierarchy to Horizontal

In chapter 4 we talk extensively about the trend toward flattening of organizational frameworks. This part of the New Compact speaks to that same issue. Its relevance to the changing nature of the business relationship is what matters here. Understanding that your prospective organization is likely to be one that has slashed layers out of its middle and is attempting to function using an empowerment model will help you persuade your prospective employer that you are a self-starter who doesn't expect to be led around by those above you in the hierarchy.

Power Interviewing Implications

Demonstrating to your prospective employer that you know how to navigate the ambiguous waters of a flattened organization will instill confidence. Employers are looking for people who can stand the heat and who can work in organizations that don't have clear lines of authority with explicit narrow job descriptions. Conveying to the interviewer that you can work independently yet cooperatively will serve your chances well of being seen as flexible and adaptable in the turbulent organization of the 21st century.

Shift 4: From the Activity Ethic to the Performance Ethic

This shift from valuing activity to valuing performance has implications if you tend to describe your history in terms of things you have done. If describing events is your primary means of conveying your experience, as it is for many people, you are missing one of the key tenets of the new compact.

Power Interviewing Implications

When interviewing, keep in mind that it is how you performed that matters to the interviewer, not just what you've done. What matters most here is that when you describe events and activities from your work history, don't forget to tell the interviewer what he or she really cares about: what impact or results your efforts had and how did that impact or those results make a difference to the company.

Shift 5: From Intentions Measured to Results Measured

Years ago attitude was an important measure in the workplace. Someone who had the right attitude could be assured of employment regardless of whether he or she was producing. Anyone who projected good intent could expect the same from an employer. This is not to say that good intent no longer counts; however, it no longer carries the clout it once used to. This shift in the New Compact suggests that your intent, pure as it may be, matters less to the interviewer and the prospective employer than the results you'll achieve for them.

Power Interviewing Implications

In the organization of the 21st century the well-meaning but low-achieving employee will not be as valued or tolerated as in the past. Long-term mutual loyalty has in many quarters been replaced by short-term mutual commitment to shared goals. The increased mobility of the workforce means that those doing the interviewing are less concerned about your intention to contribute in the long run than about your ability to deliver results immediately.

Shift 6: From Employer as Parent to Employer as Partner

Of all the shifts manifested in the New Compact this is perhaps the one that most exemplifies the changing nature of the relationship between the individual and the organization. The shift from the organization as the primary caretaker of the employee and his or her career to a relationship whereby the employee manages his or her own career in partnership with the organization has many implications.

Power Interviewing Implications

The worst thing you can do to sabotage the interviewer's comfort level is to suggest, deliberately or by implication, that you expect the organization to take care of you once you come on board. Implicit in the New Compact is the expectation that you understand that you are responsible for your career and that the company at best will play a supporting role in the management of your career.

Shift 7: From a Compliance Strategy to a Commitment Strategy

This shift is particularly important to be aware of if you are applying for a management position. Compliance as a managerial strategy has gone the way of the buggy whip. Managers who cling to an old-fashioned command-and-control style of management find themselves hopelessly without influence over the independent, self-empowered workers of the new workforce. The reality is that in a fast-paced, highly volatile, ever-changing marketplace where loyalty to an organization is increasingly rare, savvy managers realize that the real influence they have comes from their capacity to build mutual commitment with the people they manage.

Power Interviewing Implications

Understanding the subtle shift from compliance to commitment as a managerial strategy can hold a real key for the well-prepared management-level applicant. Interviewers these days know that one of the trickiest aspects of managing in an organization is tapping into the motivation of those being managed. An interviewee can make a tremendously positive impression by articulating an understanding of the shift from compliance to commitment. This shift isn't easy, particularly for seasoned applicants who have been schooled in the command-and-control approach. However, demonstrating an appreciation for the need to build mutual commitment will assure your interviewer that you are not a dinosaur.

Shift 8: From Manager as Controller to Manager as Coach

Many large corporations are expending enormous resources to teach their current managers how to make this shift. Among the most popular management development courses today are courses on coaching skills. These courses are designed to teach managers how to create the managerial shift from compliance to commitment. For example, managers are taught how to listen better so that they can build commitment between themselves and those around them. They are taught how to help others become problem solvers rather than merely solve problems for them. And they are taught how to become teachers and guides of others' development.

Power Interviewing Implications

In the interest of presenting yourself as someone whose hand is on the pulse of contemporary organizational life, you had better—if you want to be seen as current in your thinking—be able to talk about your capacity to coach and your understanding of the limits of controlling others. If you want to score points as a strong managerial applicant, make sure you convey a deep understanding of what it takes to effectively coach others and how those coaching skills help you to build commitment and strengthen your influence on those around you.

Leveraging the New Compact

Understanding the New Compact will vary from interview to interview depending on the sophistication of your interviewer. Some interviewers will be keenly aware of the eight shifts discussed herein, others less so. Whether your interviewer has a clear view of these shifts is not something you are likely to know going into the interview unless you have good inside information on who the interviewer is and what makes him or her tick. However, you can be sure that those who are charged with finding the best and the brightest for organizations are at some level aware of these shifts. The extent to which you can paint a picture of yourself as someone who understands the changes taking place in organizations, and as someone who is prepared to respond to the New Compact, will determine the extent to which you are seen as someone who has what it takes to make a significant contribution to the future of any organization.

LEARNING ABOUT THE EMPLOYER

In addition to preparing your personal strategy for your performance in the interview, you need some information about the company you're approaching. Anyone going into an interview without having done his or her homework is at a distinct disadvantage from the beginning and will remain in that position throughout the selection process.

If the company you're approaching is publicly held, chances are its stock is traded on a major exchange like the New York Stock Exchange or NASDAQ. These companies are required by law to publish and make available at no cost their annual and financial disclosure reports, which are an excellent source of information and will help you during the interview. Within these reports you will find the following:

- Information about the principals will reveal their goals and ambitions for the company. In most successful companies you will find that the values of the leaders have trickled down into the management ranks, thus giving you valuable information about the person sitting across from you.
- Their business philosophy will tell you about their priorities, strategies, and managerial approach. This information will begin to tell you whether you're pursuing a company that is a good match for you in terms of your own priorities and way of operating.
- Their area of expertise will also tell you whether they are a good match in terms of your competencies and interests. Whereas most organizations deal with a range of products or services, they tend to have specialties. It makes sense to target organizations whose primary areas are also your primary areas of skill and interest.
- Their accomplishments will tell you how successful they are at

excelling in their area and will give you an idea of the opportunities that may present themselves if you join them.

- Their setbacks will tell you what their weaknesses are and potential areas for problems in the future. In addition, this information may suggest ways in which you might make a unique contribution, particularly if you have some strengths in areas that have presented problems for them in the past.
- The stability of their financial base is important information in terms of the organization's short-term future. A company on shaky ground may be a target of a takeover and may not be a good career risk. Many people have found themselves victims of a brief tenure because the company was bought out soon after they joined.
- What their current priorities are will tell you what they are likely to be focusing on in the near future. If their priorities excite you, you'll want to let that be known in the interview. If they don't excite you, you may want to look elsewhere.
- What long-term contracts the company has secured will tell you the long-range outlook for the organization. If you're looking for stability, the more long-term commitments the organization has, the better.

If the company is privately held, it is not under as much scrutiny and is not required by law to share as much information as a public company. Information may be a little harder to come by. However, gaining information remains important to the interview and to your decision, should you be faced with one, about joining the organization. Privately held companies may or may not issue annual and financial reports; if not, the following sources can help you get the information you need:

- The Better Business Bureau will probably have a listing for the company if it's privately held. The bureau can tell you if there have been any problems with its performance in relation to other companies or with consumers.
- The competition has a vested interest in your prospective organization. Chances are that if they are at all concerned with maintaining their market share, your company's competitors are

keenly aware of your target's strengths and weaknesses. Although this information must be pursued diplomatically, it is actually quite easy to gain information through this channel. An interesting side benefit may well be the discovery of another potential employer.

- The chamber of commerce is perhaps the organization most committed to the concept of networking. In fact, for many chambers, networking is one of the primary functions. Talking to someone in the chamber will shed light on your prospective company, and may also lead to some valuable introductions. People who represent their companies through the chamber make it their business to promote their company. While you may have to sort the substantive from the propaganda, you can get a great deal from tapping this resource. Keep in mind that there are two sorts of chamber contacts, those who represent the chamber as an organization and those who represent individual companies. The former are good for information about companies and the general market in their area, and the latter for contacts and introductions.

- Current employees are the best source of information about the inner workings of a company. No one knows better what working in a place is like than someone who works there. Approaching people in your prospective company can be worth the effort. If you're approaching a large company, you may want to be inconspicuous and start by talking with people somewhat removed from your potential work site. If you're approaching a smaller organization, you may have to be more careful and ask for confidentiality. Getting introduced to someone who's known for discretion is best if possible. In any event, spending time with people who work where you want to work can help you get a better feel for the place and help you gauge your performance once you get an actual interview.

- Type and style of advertising can tell you a great deal about a prospective employer. Paying attention to the ways in which the company promotes its services and products will give you a feel for its marketing approach and priorities. In general, the slicker the advertising, the more concerned the company is with image and the image it wants its employees to project. Paying attention to the types and amount of advertising your targeted company is doing can tell you how well it's doing, what the market is, what value it sees in its products, and what it would like the public to think.

STRESS AND THE INTERVIEW

Depending on the type of organization you're approaching and the type of person the interviewer is, you will encounter varying degrees of stress in the interview process. Although stress interviews for the most part have gone the way of the horse buggy, stress questions are still fairly common. Less common, but reported occasionally, are stress situations, situations created to see how the applicant responds to a set of difficult circumstances.

For example, there's a classic interviewing film made by the army. In it the interviewee enters the interviewer's office and takes a seat. Shortly thereafter the interviewer asks the interviewee if he wouldn't mind opening the window. The interviewee begins struggling with a window that is nailed shut. The interviewee is then assessed on how he responded, and assumptions are made on how he would respond on the job.

The stated purpose of the film is to show interviewers how to assess an applicant's stress performance. Most interviewers today would agree that this artificial exercise tells little about how a person would respond on the job. Although the classic stress situation is rarely used today, a variation of it exists in what's often called an assessment interview. An applicant may be given a situation to manage comparable to one that might come up at work. Typically, assessment situations, like the old-fashioned stress situation, are a little more stressful than real-life situations.

The important thing to remember when facing stress in an interview, whether it be questions that seem impossible to answer or situations that seem overly difficult to solve, is that your stress performance is what counts. How you respond to stress questions or stressful situations is more important than the response you give or the solution you come up with.

Remember, when you start to feel increasingly stressed, what counts is not that you put out the fire but that you show you can stand the heat.

Interview Performance Anxiety

Performance anxiety comes in two forms: preperformance or midstream. It has to do with nervousness that overcomes a person before or during an activity. Actors call it stage fright. In its preperformance form, people feel a sense of panic that they can no longer produce what they've prepared for. Actors may forget their lines, not remember entry points, or fear they lack the talent necessary to succeed. Midstream performance anxiety has to do with loss of confidence and ability in the middle of an activity. A tennis player who double-faults on a serve and then proceeds to lose a series of games, a runner who stumbles and fails to regain momentum, a quarterback who gets sacked early in a game and subsequently fails to complete any passes, are examples of midstream performance anxiety.

Preperformance anxiety can occur just before an interview and can be debilitating. For example, a bad day at work the day before an interview can trigger a lack of self-confidence and result in poor performance the next day. An unresolved argument at home the night before an interview can have the same effect. Even wearing clothes that feel uncomfortable or don't fit well can create preperformance anxiety.

During an interview, midstream performance anxiety can be triggered in many ways. Being asked an unanticipated question can produce anxiety. Reading the interviewer's nonverbal behavior in a negative way can create problems. Distractions such as phone calls and interruptions in the flow of conversation can throw the interviewee into a panic.

When confronted with performance anxiety before an interview, the important thing is to resolve or get rid of whatever it is that is causing the anxiety. Changing your clothes, resolving conflicts, cleaning up messes on the job before leaving will reduce your anxiety and improve your performance.

When confronted with performance anxiety during an interview, the important thing is to recognize it early, overcome it, and regain composure. For example, some actors' strategy for overcoming stage fright resulting from the size or makeup of an audience is to find one person in the crowd who looks friendly and inviting and to play to that person as though he or she were the only person in the audience. This would be a good strategy to remember for a group interview (a frequent cause of performance anxiety). Identify the one person in the room who seems most receptive and least threatening and play to that person.

One common mistake that often triggers interview performance anxiety is the perception on the part of the applicant that whatever happens in the room is directly related to the interview. Applicants read all sorts of things into the interviewer's behavior that can cause an anxiety reaction. Remember that interviewers have a lot on their minds besides your performance. As long as you're presenting yourself in the best light possible, chances are good you will make a positive impression. Sometimes remembering not to worry can be the best remedy to interview performance anxiety.

One strategy many athletes use to overcome midstream performance anxiety is to visualize themselves succeeding in the very act in which they just fumbled. The quarterback might envision himself throwing a touchdown pass; the runner, tearing through the ribbon at the finish line; the tennis player, taking the set. One thing you might try in an interview in which you are fumbling is to imagine yourself receiving the offer, or better yet, arriving for your first day on the job.

Whatever approach you take, be aware of the possibility of performance anxiety affecting you both before and during an interview. Interviews are nerve-racking experiences by design. You don't need the burden of performance anxiety to tax you further. Do what you need to do to avoid and shed performance anxiety and you will undoubtedly do better in the interview—and get more offers.

WHEN THEY JUST SAY NO

A classic skit from the early nineties *Tracy Ullman Show* vividly illustrates the way the interview process works—and why the best candidate doesn't always get the job. The skit takes place in a corporate conference room. Three applicants (a man and two women) have just been told that they are equally qualified for a position. For a final decision each candidate is asked by the woman interviewing them to do something creative for one minute with "the magic box." The magic box is an old wooden filing drawer filled with a variety of items including clothespins, dental floss, a carpenter's saw, four full soda bottles, wooden dowels, bandages, and a cap gun with exploding caps.

The male applicant goes first and begins frantically rummaging through the magic box. As time is about to run out on his minute he desperately grabs two clothespins, places them on his lips, and quacks like a duck. Disappointed in his performance, he sits down. Tracy is next. She pins up her skirt with the two clothespins, removes the bottle caps, and pounds them into the soles of her shoes. Next she takes the exploding caps from the toy gun and places them around the top edges of the boardroom table. She then jumps on the table and does an elaborate song and dance, tapping her way over the exploding caps for accompaniment. Pleased with her performance, she sits down.

The next woman, the final candidate, walks gracefully over to the magic box, takes the dental floss, and fastens it to both ends of an 18-inch dowel. She picks up the carpenter's saw, returns to her seat, and plays a tonally perfect rendition of "Over the Rainbow," playing the flossed dowel against the saw as though it were a violin and bow.

After the three performances, the woman making the decision bypasses the two female candidates, who clearly outperformed the man, and congratulates him on winning the job. After the two disgruntled women leave, the interviewer confronts her new charge and tells him there are two reasons he got the job. "First," she says, "you could never be a threat to my position, and second, I don't find you the least bit sexually attractive."

Aside from the humor and sexual role reversal displayed in this skit, the scenario points to a key aspect of the interview process, the notion of rejection. If you are rejected after an interview, try not to take it personally. So devastated are some people that it takes them weeks if not months to recover and begin seeking other interviews. Keep in mind that the interview process is a flawed one and that often the reasons for your rejection have nothing to do with you or your performance. Like the characters in the skit, you are subject to variables beyond your control. Prepare as well as you can; perform your best; take rejection as their loss, not yours; and move on to your winning interview.

HANDLING DISCRIMINATION

Another aspect of the story of the magic box is discrimination. Regardless of who you are, you are vulnerable to discrimination. Whether it's your sex, your age, your race, or some less overt factor, you may be discriminated against in the selection process. Although there are laws to protect applicants against some forms of discrimination, the reality is that discriminatory acts are committed in interviews every day in all sorts of organizations.

Handling discrimination in an interview can be tricky. If someone asks you an illegal question that you believe is intended to elicit information that could be used against you (for example, questions about your marital status, age, or ethnic background), you have several choices. You can answer the question and hope the information is not used against you. You can refuse to answer the question on the grounds that it is private information. You can point out that the question is illegal and lodge a formal complaint. You can bring suit against the interviewer, claiming discrimination.

As you can see, the responses range from the compliant to the litigious. The response you choose to take should be based on your own moral values and your desire to work in that organization. Most likely, the more confrontational you are in your response to a potentially discriminating question, the less likely you are to be asked to work in that organization. Some people, offended by a certain question but anxious to work in the organization, would respond cooperatively during an interview but would voice their disapproval at the illegal question once they are part of the organization and in a more influential position. Others decide not to pursue work in a given organization because of its discriminatory attitudes. Others feel a moral obligation to fight discrimination whenever it arises and feel compelled to fight it either through a formal complaint or a legal challenge.

Handling discrimination is a personal matter, one that does not lend itself to prescription. As a job candidate you need to be aware of its possibility and you need to be ready to respond in a way that feels most appropriate to you, given the particular circumstances, your own moral standards, and your motivation for procuring the job.

WHEN TO PULL OUT THE STOPS

While most interviews are like walking a tightrope—the goal being to get to the other end—on occasion a different metaphor is appropriate. If you're applying for a job for which the competition is wide open, you need to put in a steady, careful performance. However, occasionally you'll find yourself in the position of being part of a pool of interviewees for a job that is already filled. You may be wondering why busy professionals would waste their time in such a case. There are several reasons. They may be trying to present an image of fairness. They may be meeting affirmative action requirements. They may be trying to keep their inside candidate in suspense. For whatever reasons, finding yourself in an interview when the decision has already been made is unfortunate. However, there are ways to take advantage of the situation.

One man we know was applying for a job as director of finance for a medium-sized company. On his way into the interview he noticed the name of a man on the directory whose title was acting director of finance. He got a sinking feeling that the interview would be a waste of time. He assumed, accurately, that unless the acting director was a real turkey, the job was probably not really available.

During the interview he looked for signs to support his fears. After receiving several signals that the job was not open, including several comments about what a good job the acting director was doing and a decided lack of attentiveness by the interviewer, he decided to take a risk. As he tells it, this is what he said: "It seems to me that you've got a really good inside candidate for this job, and unless I'm mistaken he's clearly the front runner. I'm sure I could do this job well, but if I were in this other man's shoes I'd feel pretty confident. I wonder if there are any other positions in this organization that you might consider me for or suggest I go after."

Now, some of you may be thinking that this man was foolish and took a big risk. You'd be right if he had made his move on a whim. However, if his judgment told him he was in a dead-end interview, he had nothing to lose and everything to gain.

In this man's case he was channeled (or as he put it, he networked his way) to another division, where he was offered a very good position.

The moral of the story: When the tightrope is taken, you may want to try the trapeze.

PERSISTENCE AND STAYING CLOSE TO THE INTERVIEWER

Don't get confused by what sounds like guidelines for salespeople rather than job candidates. Because interviewing is so much like sales—you are the product—we will from time to time borrow advice from sales experts. One piece of advice is important. You need to remind the interviewer of your interest in the job, you need to ask for the job, and you need to pursue the job until it is no longer available.

I once interviewed twenty people for an opening. After two sets of interviews the selection narrowed to two candidates. One candidate had a strong background and interviewed well, but he never asked for the job and was not overtly enthusiastic. The other candidate had less experience and was not quite as smooth in the interview. However, she was very enthusiastic and specifically asked for the job, twice. Before I made the hiring decision I replayed the interviews in my mind; my choice was to hire the positive, aggressive candidate. Her persistence was what I remember most about those interviews.

Just as the salesperson has to ask for the order, you have to ask for the job. While you should not be obnoxious in the pursuit of a position, you want to make it clear to the interviewer that you are interested in the job and believe that you are a good match. Asking for the job in the interview and in subsequent contacts you have with the potential employer is a good idea. Remember, most people have a lot on their minds other than filling the position you want. If you ask them for it and they were leaning somewhat toward you anyway, they just might say yes.

WHO'S THE BOSS?

We've known of more than one occasion when new employees arrived on the job to find that they'd be working for someone they never met during the interview process. This can be particularly unsettling if part of the applicant's decision to take the job was based on a presumed reporting relationship. Since the superior-subordinate relationship can be the linchpin of a good job, it is critical to know who's in charge. This information is easy to find out: If it's not offered in the course of the interview, simply ask before making a commitment.

It is also wise to look beyond the immediate superior and find out what the chain of command is between you and the top. This can be helpful for several reasons. It can tell you at what level you'd be entering the organization, and it can also indicate how many steps up are available to you. Beyond that, it can give you clues about how valued your unit and function are to the company brass.

In general, those positions considered most critical to the organization's leaders have a minimum of intermediaries between the top and the particular employee. If the chain of command between you and the chief executive officer (CEO) has a multitude of links, you're probably not too highly valued. The closer you are to the base of power, the more valued you are—and the greater the opportunities will be.

THE OTHER SIDE OF THE FENCE

An important thing to remember is that interviewers have a lot at stake in the interviewing process. Companies lose millions of dollars every year because of poor hiring decisions. Although interviewers may not have as much at stake as interviewees, their reputation, the productivity of their unit, and in some cases their jobs depend on choosing and hiring the right people for the right jobs. While different organizations approach the process in different ways, it is likely that any organization you get offers from will take you through at least two steps, the initial screening interview, and the in-depth interview. It is helpful, in getting a full picture of the interview process, to look at the situation from the interviewer's side of the fence. After reviewing the interviewing procedures of many companies, we have devised the following review of the interview process from the perspective of the interviewer: first of the objectives of the initial interview, and then of the steps likely to occur in any interview. This will give you a bird's-eye view of the interviewer's priorities to ensure that you meet his or her needs.

Objectives of the Initial Interview
(from the Interviewer's Perspective)

The interview is a way to obtain information about a candidate in a limited time period. At its best it is a complete and succinct process of evaluation. At its worst it is an unfocused conversation that yields little helpful information. The key to successful interviewing is the interviewer's ability to focus the interview by being clear about the needs of the organization and becoming familiar with the qualifications of the candidate.

The interview is used to discover the candidate's likelihood of success by probing his or her background. A candidate's patterns of involvement; achievement; and success at work, in school, and socially are patterns that will be repeated in the business environment. This premise, that a person's potential for success can be determined by an analysis of his or her background, is the basis for the decision of whether or not the candidate should be given further consideration.

In the interview it is necessary to:

- Discover and evaluate the candidate's history in light of the corporation's predetermined requirements.
- Evaluate those elements that can be determined in a face-to-face meeting (business presence, appearance, personality, and communication skills).
- Provide candidates with general information about the corporation and specific information about the job for which the candidate is interviewing.

The key steps are:

- Review background of candidate.
- Evaluate patterns of success.
- Test for key traits and characteristics.
- Observe behavior during the interview.
- Make a decision to take candidate to next step or reject.

Steps in the Interview Process
(from the Interviewer's Perspective)

1. *Review résumé (before interview).* Look for patterns of growth and outstanding accomplishments, or lack of growth and lack of accomplishments. Note items to be pursued. Also check career objectives.
2. *Greet candidate and establish rapport.* Do what's necessary (within reason) to make the applicant feel welcomed and relatively relaxed.
3. *Confirm candidate's interest in the corporation and explain agenda.* Explain to the candidate that he or she will be asked some questions, that information about the corporation and specific job opportunities will be presented, and that he or she will be given a chance to ask questions.
4. *Probe for key characteristics.* The purpose of probes is to ask applicants to expand on information provided in the résumé. In addition, probes give candidates the opportunity to demonstrate verbal ability, organization, confidence, and poise. Probes should be sufficiently broad in scope to require the applicants to analyze their own thoughts and expand on personal experience; for example, "Tell me more about your role in this project." Remember, there is little value in simply rehashing information provided in the candidate's résumé.
5. *Provide a brief overview of the corporation.*

   • Discuss in general how the applicant's experience and academic training might fit into the organization, including possible career paths and work locations. Be careful, however, not to create unrealistic expectations.
   • Describe the corporation from your perspective by pointing out how specific policies, benefits, and philosophies have affected your career.
   • Stress what is unique about this corporation rather than what is common to most business organizations.

6. *Solicit questions.* Clear up questions the candidate has and also substantiate your evaluation of the applicant's interest in employment with the corporation. (If the candidate has no questions about the organization or the job, suspect a lack of interest.)

7. *Close the interview.* Be explicit. The candidate should be informed that his or her qualifications will be reviewed by managers in light of current and/or anticipated openings. After the management review, the next step, if appropriate, may be an invitation to the corporation or a branch office for further interviews. In every case make it clear to the candidates that they will hear from the corporation within a reasonable period. Never reject applicants in an interview or leave them with the impression that they will probably receive a job offer.

8. *Complete evaluation forms.* Record your impressions of the candidate immediately, because your perceptions of that person will never be more clear. Try to make a decision now.

These are steps likely to be taken in the screening, or initial, interview. Subsequent interviews are far less predictable and vary in scope and content. The interviewer's style, the culture of the organization, and the nature of the position will determine how subsequent interviews are held.

For example, Harvey MacKay, president of MacKay Envelopes and author of *Swim with the Sharks Without Being Eaten Alive,* has a unique approach—and the lowest turnover rate in his industry. MacKay and his staff go through an elaborate selection process for everyone in the organization. It takes anywhere from two months to three years to fill key positions. What MacKay does is get to know applicants extremely well through interviews with the candidates, their families, and even their neighbors. He then spends time with the candidate, doing a variety of things including leisure activities of the applicant's choice.

While this unconventional approach may seem a bit exaggerated for some of you (although some of you no doubt would welcome it), it illustrates the way some companies handle the selection process.

Regardless of the approach your interviewer takes, the way to have a successful in-depth interview is to prepare yourself by studying the seven key evaluation factors, the twelve trends to take you over the top, and the strategies for making the all-important connection, outlined in Chapters 2 through 5.

INTERVIEWING FOR JOBS IN SMALL BUSINESSES

There is no way to predict what kind of interview you will have, but there are some predictable patterns. What has been covered in this chapter so far applies to all types of organizations, but there is a category that is so often overlooked by the job seeker that we choose to highlight it here. When searching for work, most people approach the obvious organizations, the high-profile companies whose names everyone is familiar with. By doing so they are overlooking the "hidden economy."

The hidden economy consists of millions of smaller firms, the vast majority of which are privately held, publish little information about their activities, and rarely appear in the business press. Since 1980 the hidden economy has created more jobs in the United States than have been created in Japan and Europe. Here are a few statistics to show what job shopping in the small business market offers.

- From 1980 to 1987 the non-Fortune 500 economy created 17 million jobs. During that same time the Fortune 500 eliminated 3.1 million people from payrolls. This is the equivalent of laying off the entire workforce of Massachusetts. In the ten years following, 1987 to 1997, the trend toward small business growth and Fortune 500 downsizing has continued. While indications are that large companies are slowly beginning to reenlist some of those they had released, the data suggests that it is the small-business sector that will continue to be the highest-growth segment of the marketplace into the next century.
- Ninety-seven percent of the businesses in the United States have fewer than 100 employees. This represents approximately 12 million firms, whereas there are only 250,000 firms with more than 100 employees.
- Two out of three workers get their first jobs with small businesses.

The good news is that the small-business market is vibrant, it is growing rapidly, and it holds tremendous opportunity for job seekers. The bad news is that finding these jobs and preparing to interview for them is more difficult than with larger companies, because:

- Most of these companies are privately rather than publicly owned.
- Many of them do not publish financial information such as annual reports.
- Job descriptions in these companies are seldom well defined.
- The interview process tends to be much more informal.

The Question of Stability

Many people shy away from small businesses because they fear the instability of an organization not protected by large numbers. However, statistics show that in the 1980s and 1990s fewer people were laid off in small companies than in large ones. This does not mean that you have nothing to fear with the small business; you do need to be careful. When approaching a small organization you want to look into its stability by asking questions about its future and making some judgments about the chances of being fired. One of the advantages to keep in mind—the plus side of the lack of stability—is the opportunity that small businesses afford for moving up in the organization. While large organizations are reducing the ranks of their upper-level people, small organizations often look to insiders to carry more of the responsibility. Consequently, if you pick the right small business you may find yourself moving up faster than you ever could in a large organization.

Getting the Interview

Networking is even more important with small businesses. Tell everyone you know you are looking for work and that you want to work for a small company. Because of their informal approach, small companies are often more responsive to networking. If you know someone in one of these companies, ask that person to help you get an interview. Because the companies are small, most employees know the people who do the hiring and are able to get their attention. Also, it is often a feather in their cap if they help get a good candidate in the door.

Check the bulletin boards and placement offices of the community colleges in the area. Many small companies look for employees by using these sources. Check the newspaper listings more carefully for jobs in these companies. Even the part-time listings can sometimes lead to full-time positions.

Use prospecting interviews more extensively. Again, these organizations have a harder time finding good people because fewer people know about them; consequently they are more responsive to people who approach them for inquiries and/or jobs.

The Interview

You should approach an interview with a small business using the strategies for power interviewing already outlined in this book; however, there are a few modifications.

Since you may not have as much information on these companies, you will have to get a better understanding of the company and the opportunity by asking questions. Make a list ahead of time of all the things you'd like to know about the company and the job and bring it to the interview. Small organizations don't expect you to be as well briefed on them as large ones do. Your questions should include, among others, the following:

- What is the company's history of sales, profits, and employee growth for the last three years?
- What are the company's goals and direction? Does it have a plan and a vision for the future?
- What would be the career path for the job you are seeking?
- Why is this job available? Is it a new position created by growth or is it available because of the promotion or termination of the person who previously held the job? A conversation with that person could be very helpful as an indicator of job requirements and expectations. It could also give you a perspective on the culture of the company.

Finally, remember that smaller companies are less likely to have jobs that are very specific or that have well-defined responsibilities. They often require employees capable of a wide range of duties. The key may be your flexibility, your ability to adapt to whatever the company's needs are. You may want to stress this in your interview along with your desire to learn and grow in the small-company environment.

SUMMARY

This chapter has covered the basics of power interviewing. Although much of what was said may seem like common sense to you, we all know how uncommon common sense is in actual practice. Consider the advice in this chapter as a base for your performance, and you're on your way to mastering the power interview.

POWER PREP STRATEGY I

What are you going to wear to the interview? _____

_____

_____

Are there any things you need that you don't have? If so, what? When are you
going to get them? _____

_____

_____

Is your résumé professionally printed? If not, when and where are you going
to have it done? _____

_____

_____

What do you know about this employer?

    Business philosophy _____

_____

    Areas of expertise _____

_____

    Accomplishments _____

_____

    Setbacks _____

_____

Financial stability _____

_____

Current priorities _____

_____

Long-term contracts _____

_____

If possible, get answers to the preceding seven items before entering the employment interview.

What is the salary range for this position? _____

_____

What is your desired salary for this position? _____

_____

What is the minimum salary you would accept? _____

_____

What benefits do you require to accept this position? _____

_____

What perks would you like to receive in addition to basic benefits? _____

_____

How much vacation time do you want? _____

_____

What is the minimum amount of vacation time you will accept? _____

_____

What aspects of this interview make you feel the most nervous? _____

_____

What can you do to get over the nervousness before the interview (for example, practice tough questions or talk with someone about your anxiety)? ____

_____

_____

_____

When will you set aside some time to do these things before the interview?

_____

_____

2

The Winning Profile: The Seven Key Evaluation Factors

If you have decided to use this book, you probably see yourself as a winner or a potential winner. You have decided to use all your personal resources, your personal power, to conduct a power interview, one that will ensure the most possible offers for the best possible jobs. By so doing you have set your sights high. To achieve your goal you need to be clear about what you have to offer and what the companies you wish to work for want. You also need to know what to do to convince the people who hire in those companies that you are a good match.

Over the years we have learned a great deal about creating matches between prospective employees and the best employers. In this chapter we will outline what the people who have the hiring power consider to be the most important assets for prospective employees.

We have narrowed these assets down to seven variables, what we call the seven key evaluation factors. What follows is a discussion of the seven factors, what they look like in action, and what you can do to convince someone that you possess them. There are many ways to show that you have the key characteristics. One of the best ways is to draw from your past. Your ability to convey your use of these traits in action will greatly enhance your performance. Telling stories illustrating your past success in using each of these traits can be very convincing. To show how this is done for each category we will present a trigger story. These are stories that have successfully convinced interviewers that the storytellers have a particular trait. The trigger stories are told in the first person to demonstrate how they can be used.

FACTOR 1

Aggressiveness and Enthusiasm

People with this factor are self-confident and self-assured. The way they present themselves, the language they use, the stories they tell to illustrate their success indicate that they are high achievers. They are people who make it clear that a significant contribution to their organization is a top priority in their lives. They are not afraid to show their enthusiasm or their willingness to compete. Because of increased global competition and much talk about America's crisis in productivity, it is imperative for the applicant to demonstrate a high level of energy and a strong commitment to company goals and priorities. By choosing to pursue work in the corporate world you make a statement about your goals and priorities. While many companies are increasingly aware of the needs of their employees and the importance of responding to those needs, the essential point in hiring is "What can this person do for this company?" The corporate recruiter is looking for someone who has drive and ambition, someone out to prove how good he or she really is. Along with the drive to excel, the successful applicant must demonstrate enthusiasm for the company's product or service. Think for a moment of a good salesperson you know, someone who's really good at selling. One thing you've probably noticed is that he or she believes, or at least seems to believe, in the product or service sold.

Since enthusiasm is a key evaluation factor, it makes sense for you to pursue work that deals with a product or service that excites you. Feigning enthusiasm is a lot harder than projecting real enthusiasm. At first you may think this limits your options, but it doesn't really. There are many companies from which to choose. If you're aiming high, chances are the company you've chosen became successful by producing a high-quality product or service. All you need to do is find companies that produce and sell things you're interested in, make sure they're the best at what they do, and let your enthusiasm pour out. One thing to keep in mind is that enthusiasm is contagious. I once had a student who was a regional distribution manager for a large restaurant chain. This man was so enthusiastic about the quality of food being produced at his restaurants that after listening to him talk about it a few times I found myself stopping at those restaurants more frequently and admiring their quality. The point is that his genuine expression of enthusiasm convinced me that his was a high-quality product and that he was doing an excellent job.

In addition to a sense of enthusiasm about the product or service of your target companies, you need to express a general enthusiasm for work. If you're looking for a job that gives you the time and freedom to pursue outside interests, the corporate world is not for you. To convince those doing the hiring that you are a good match for them, you must convey a sense of determination, a willingness to go the extra mile for the company. If you're not willing to, it will be difficult to convince someone that you're right for the position. That someone probably won't hire you, and is probably doing you a favor.

Trigger Story One of the periods I'm most proud of is the time I started working at InfoTech. I was hired as an assistant marketing manager to help in the development and launching of their new personal computer. After I was there about two weeks the marketing manager had a heart attack. As you can imagine, that threw the project into a tailspin. Management immediately started talking about pushing the project back for six months. I thought about it that night, and realized that in the fast-paced personal computer market six months would spell disaster. I decided I would do what I could to fend off the potential loss.

The next morning I went in to talk with the vice-president in charge of our division. I told him that I was concerned that a six-month delay would cause irreparable damage to our product line. I also told him that I thought we had the best product out there and that given a timely release we could capture a good part of the market. He agreed and started lamenting about what a blow the marketing manager's illness was to the company (not to mention to the marketing manager).

At that point I interrupted him and told him I had a plan. I took out the outline I had worked on the night before showing how with a little reorganizing I could pick up some of the marketing manager's responsibilities until he was able to return. I sketched out a plan that involved my dropping some of my current tasks, giving them to someone else, and picking up the key tasks of my boss. I told him there were some new things I would have to learn but that none of them seemed overwhelming. I let him know I was willing to do whatever it took to make this work. He reluctantly agreed to make me acting marketing manager for this project. The next six months were unbelievable. I learned a lot and worked constantly. We had a successful first season and our product eventually became a big seller.

FACTOR 2

Communication Skills

As the world, and particularly the U.S. corporation, becomes entrenched in the information age, the importance of effective communication cannot be overstated. If information is power, then those who communicate best are the most powerful.

One aspect of the emergence of the information age is the transition of the U.S. economy to a service economy. So pervasive is this shift that one major Fortune 500 company recently announced it was shifting its emphasis from a production-based computer company to a service-based company. Since quality service depends on the ability to communicate with the customer, a prospective employee's ability to communicate becomes paramount.

Being able to communicate means being able to convey information, ideas, and attitudes lucidly and persuasively. In an age where scarcely a day goes by without reports in the media on the failure of schools to produce literate graduates, effective communication skills are highly prized in the marketplace. Prospective employers want to see that you not only have basic competence in speaking and writing clearly but excel in this area. Your ability to demonstrate that you have superior communication skills and that you can effectively influence others through the written and spoken word will greatly increase your chances.

You need to be prepared to demonstrate your communication skills in an interview. You will be judged by the extent to which you communicate clearly and effectively. Unless you're asked to produce a writing sample (more companies are doing this), you may be evaluated only on your oral communication skills. Here you will be examined for your ability both to process and to convey information. Your ability to demonstrate command of the English language will take you far in the interview process. However, beyond mastery of the language, your performance in the interview should also demonstrate your ability to manage the communication process. If in the course of an interview there is an incident of faulty communication (more often than not, there is) this is an ideal opportunity to demonstrate your abilities. Don't be afraid to clarify what you've said if it was misunderstood, or to ask for clarification if what you've been told or asked is unclear. Most people won't do this in an interview; however, demonstrating a commitment to and an affinity for clear communication will make you stand out from the crowd.

Trigger Story One of the most exciting experiences in my work life was when I was asked to prepare and deliver a speech in front of five hundred managers. I had been working for Premium Manufacturing and had gotten involved in an employee participation program. A group of us were meeting on a weekly basis to try and iron out some production problems. Because I was a vocal member of the group during the early stages I was asked to be the chair. Since I had never done this before I didn't know how to proceed. I bought a book on running meetings and had things moving pretty smoothly within a few weeks.

Eventually my group was able to make some real changes in the production process. Through our discussions we were able to cut production time by 20 percent in several areas and devised a way to reduce the number of rejected pieces by 30 percent. The plant manager was so impressed with our results that he asked me to make a presentation at a national meeting of company managers. I agreed to do it. When he told me I would be talking to a group of nearly five hundred managers I thought I was going to collapse. I had never spoken in front of more than twenty-five people at a time.

I got a few books on public speaking and began talking with people who had done some. Eventually I got more comfortable with the idea. I spent a good deal of time preparing for the presentation, writing extensive notes on cards. When the time came to speak I was pretty nervous, but well prepared. In fact, when I actually gave the speech I hardly looked at my notes. When I was done several people approached me and told me what a good job I had done. I've since been asked to speak at several conferences. I still get nervous, but it gets easier every time.

FACTOR 3

Record of Success

Since most successful companies pride themselves on being the best, it makes sense to assume that they will hire only people who they believe are the best at what they do. You may be highly trained and capable of performing at an excellent level, but unless you have a history of success you will have a hard time gaining access to the companies you most want.

Most people interested in good corporate jobs have respectable track records. The problem is that many people cannot explain their success. If you can define the reasons for your success, you can transfer these traits to the skills and characteristics necessary for the job you want. When you discuss your success be sure to delineate your role in the activity. For example, if you chaired a successful fund-raising campaign, state how your presence made a difference and was an integral part of the project's success. The key here is being able to translate previous successes into terms that get and keep the attention of your interviewer. If your past successes are similar to the kinds of challenges likely to come in your desired job, speak freely about them in the interview. If your past successes differ from anticipated challenges (say, if this is a career change or you are a new graduate), don't despair; just be ready to describe the relevance of past successes to the work ahead.

The important thing in conveying a record of success is to present yourself in a way that highlights your uniqueness. Too many people resort to hackneyed expressions that sound all too familiar to the interviewer. It's important to remember that interviewers hear the same responses over and over. The best approach is to tell some vivid, relevant stories about your past successes that set you apart from the crowd. In telling your success stories remember that the interviewer is most interested in your unique contribution to a problem's resolution. In addition, keep in mind that the stories you choose to tell say something about your record of success, and they also reveal what's important to you.

Trigger Story One of the areas that's always interested me is leadership. Figuring out how to get people to do things and making a group work toward a common end have always been challenging. Ever since

I was a kid I took whatever opportunities I could find to play a leadership role. I've been involved with a lot of sports teams and was captain of the track team in junior high and high school. Once I got into college I decided to pursue academics more than sports—I had some injuries that prevented me from having a strong college career in sports so I didn't want to waste my time. I got involved in politics pretty heavily: I ran for president of the student senate and won two years in a row. What those experiences did was teach me that I liked to lead people and that I was pretty good at it. I found that skill and interest transferring into my work life as well. In my first job I became a team leader in my division, and we outperformed the internal competition three years in a row. The thing that I like most about a leadership role is the challenge of figuring out who the people in a particular task group are and what makes them tick. Once I figure out who it is I'm working with and what motivates them, I get a real charge out of harnessing the power of the team.

FACTOR 4

Rational Thought Process

One of the most common complaints about the contemporary workforce is that today's applicants lack the ability to be critical thinkers.
As the marketplace gets more complex, the need to have employees
who can solve problems is a priority. Your ability to demonstrate your
critical thinking abilities will take you far in the interview process.
Being able to articulate what you want in a job and why you think you
can handle that sort of work will make the difference between moving
ahead and being passed over.

The astute applicant realizes that in addition to gaining information
in an interview, the corporate interviewer is also trying to get a feel for
the applicant's potential. Conveying to the interviewer that you are an
intelligent, resourceful, and highly competent person will take you a
long way in the selection process. Demonstrating an ability in the
interview to solve problems, or more important, to think in a problem-
solving mode, will impress and reassure the interviewer.

The key word here is *process*. As the business world gets more
complex and competition more fierce, leaders of corporations realize
that what they need most, throughout the organizational ranks, is people who think well. While implementation remains important, it's the
idea people who make the difference in the long run. Being able to see
new angles on old problems is highly valued, as is identifying new
problems to be tackled. It's the "tinkerers," says Harvard Business
School Professor of Leadership Abraham Zalesnik, who make the difference in the contemporary company. This sentiment is reflected in
the number of companies that create opportunities for intrapreneurs,
people whose role it is to think of new products, services, and processes for the organization. In a sense everyone in the successful company of the 1990s needs to be an intrapreneur. Emphasis on each
employee being a high-level thinker and problem solver is here to stay.
As an applicant seeking work it is to your advantage to convey an ability to think clearly, creatively, and rationally.

Trigger Story One of the most challenging situations I've been in
was when I took a job as a project manager for a small company that
had developed a new line of computer software. I had been on the job

for about a week when I became very frustrated. The president of the company, the person who hired me, had not given me any direction since our initial orientation meeting. I didn't know what I was supposed to do. I decided to go in and tell him of my frustration. We had a brief meeting at which I told him of my frustration over his lack of direction. He told me he hired me because he thought I could figure out the best way to apply my talents to the task at hand. If he'd made a mistake, he offered, we could go our separate ways and there would be no hard feelings.

After getting over the shock of almost losing my week-old job, I told him that there was no problem and that I would get going right away. I decided that the best thing I could do was figure out what needed to be done most with this product and do it—fast. I spoke with the software designers and found out that the product was ready to go to production, but that they had no idea how many to produce, they had no packaging for it, and they didn't have any marketing plans. I got hold of a planning program I had used before and developed a time line for production, design, and marketing of the product. I did some market research, spoke with some advertisers, and made some decisions on a first run of the product. Once my system was in place I found myself with plenty to do and an organized strategy for doing it.

After that things worked out very well and my tenure with that company was quite successful—and I never again asked the president what he wanted me to do.

FACTOR 5

Maturity

There is a lot of talk these days about the lack of maturity of the emerging workforce. The *New York Times* recently had an article that reported on the number of people in their twenties and thirties who were returning home to live with parents. Although some gave economics as the reason for their retreat, a large number gave responses that led the researchers to believe it was not economics but the inability to cope with the demands of modern life that brought them back home.

Imagine the worry of the corporate recruiter who reads that article. The thought of hiring someone who is living with mom and dad to avoid the harsh realities of life at the dawn of the 21st century would send shivers up one's spine.

There is a perception, articulated in popular books, movies, and other media, that the current generation has a problem in growing up. There is a concern that prolonged adolescence is a result of a generation raised in an affluent society, and that for many college has served as a way of perpetuating the irresponsibility of an entire generation.

Recruiters, burned by seemingly attractive prospects who leave a company after a few months because they can't stand the stress, are aware of the maturity problem. In seeking talent, they are increasingly concerned that the people they pick are grown up enough to handle the territory.

The best way to demonstrate you have the maturity to survive the inevitable difficulties and challenges of life in corporate America is to convey to your interviewer your sense of responsibility. Highlight past experiences that demonstrate your willingness and ability to hang in during difficult times. Demonstrate your willingness and ability to act as a leader and to gain others' confidence in your leadership. Remember, those doing the hiring don't want to raise you; they want to benefit from your having been raised well.

Trigger Story One of the most personally satisfying things I've done was help set up a crisis center in college. The idea began when some friends and I were sitting around in the dormitory. A guy down the hall was having a difficult time—we didn't know if it was a drug problem, an emotional problem, or what, but he clearly needed some help. After searching for some help on campus and off, we realized that there were no crisis services available for people in need of them. We went to the campus counseling center and asked them what if anything could be done about it. They said that they would be glad to help but that there were no funds. We went to the dean of students and told him of our concern. He was very responsive and supportive and even gave us a room and a little money to get started. With the help of the counseling center we got some outside experts to come in and meet with us. Since money was scarce we decided to try a peer counseling approach. We recruited interested students and got the experts to train us at minimal cost. Eventually we set up a 24-hour drop-in center with a crisis hotline. We did some peer counseling and a lot of referral to outside agencies. The best thing was that we now had a place that people could come any time for immediate help until they could get to a professional. The center was very successful and has become well known on campus. In recent years I have volunteered to help new students become peer counselors. I spend a couple of weekends a year each September getting the place up and running—it's a lot of fun.

Planning and Organization

As organizations continue to reduce the numbers of managers, the ability of every employee to perform managerial tasks becomes essential. As organizational hierarchies flatten out, leaving fewer middle-level managers to oversee the work, the expectation is that successful employees can manage their own work. The ability to plan and organize one's responsibilities and to monitor one's performance is greatly valued by those who hire. The extent to which an applicant can demonstrate in an interview the skills involved in planning and organizing projects will determine the interviewer's sense that the applicant can handle a high level of responsibility.

There are many approaches to planning that make sense. The important thing in an interview is to have an approach, which should include a clear strategy for analyzing problems, setting goals and objectives, creating strategies for solving problems, implementing plans, and evaluating results. Being careful to comment on each of these key variables will assure your interviewer that you understand planning and are capable of engaging in it. Being able to articulate clearly each element of the planning process will assure the interviewer that you have an organized mind and are capable of organized activity.

Trigger Story In my last job I was asked to lead the computerization of the organization's business office. It wasn't officially part of my job but I was the person in the organization who knew the most about computer systems. I was asked to manage the transition with the understanding that it would take about 20 percent of my time until completed. I was excited about the project and committed to making it as smooth a transition as possible. Since management was committed to getting the best system possible, money was no object. My two concerns were getting the best equipment and getting people through the transition with as little difficulty as possible. I knew that it would take careful planning to execute the plan smoothly.

The first thing I did was to poll the office staff to find out what their needs were and what their concerns were about the transition to computers. At the same time I had representatives from the top computer companies come in and pitch their products to me. After gathering all this information I spent some time with it, made some decisions, and drafted a proposal to management that included product choices, installation time lines, training time lines, and project completion target dates.

Once management accepted my plan I presented it to the office staff and asked for their input. I then made modifications in the plan, ran it by management one more time, and implemented it. The installation of the system, the training, and the total transition went on as scheduled with only a few minor glitches. A month after the shift was completed I did an informal survey with the office staff to see how things were going and how they felt about the transition. I was happy to see that almost all the staff felt the changes had increased their productivity and that they felt comfortable with the new system.

FACTOR 7

Reaction to Pressure

Because of increased global competition, most U.S. corporations believe that to remain on top they must constantly outdo their competitors. The typical response of the vice-president when confronted with a major success by a subordinate is "Yes, but what are you going to do for us tomorrow?" In the progressive company there is no room for resting on one's laurels. Too many organizations have gone under or lost ground by getting arrogant about success. Successful companies and employees recognize that in the accelerated pace of the contemporary marketplace, innovation and change are constant.

Those who hire are seeking people who not only can handle pressure but have ways of managing it and, at best, can thrive on it. While you can count on getting some questions on your reactions to pressure and change, it's to your advantage to discuss that aspect of modern professional life before your interviewer brings it up. It is clear that if you are bothered by pressure or change, the corporate world is not for you. Taking a positive stance on this issue early in an interview can serve you well. Showing that you can stand the heat, and may even welcome it, gives you an edge over others who merely demonstrate an ability to tolerate it. Although no one serious about getting high-prestige offers will admit to not liking pressure, taking an aggressive position on this issue can enhance your stature in the eyes of the interviewer.

Trigger Story One of the most stressful situations I was in was when I worked for a small distribution company. We were telemarketing a piece of computer software that was unique. Word was out in the industry that another company was developing a similar product to compete with ours, but it wouldn't be out for another month. The president of the company decided that the month we had prior to the release of the competitor's product could be very lucrative. He decided to hire 50 temporary people to market our software aggressively. Since I was in charge of distribution and knew the most about marketing the product, he put me in charge of hiring and training the temporary staff.

Finding people who were willing to learn to market a product for just one month was difficult. I tapped all the employment agencies in the area and developed an incentive program with bonuses for high sales. I then hired and trained the 50 operators to market and place orders. Within ten days we had our 50 people up and running. It was an intense period for me but very exciting. After a month we had met our quota. There was also an interesting break. The competition fell behind on its time line and couldn't release its product for another six weeks. We were able to retain 40 of the people we had originally hired for six weeks more and managed to outsell our initial projections by 50 percent.

SUMMARY

We have presented an outline of the factors that are key to the evaluation of candidates seeking work in corporate America. We have given you examples of achievements that reflect strengths in each category. Taken together these guidelines and examples form a profile of the ideal candidate. If you see yourself in all, or at least in most, of the factors, your chances of getting an interesting position in the corporate sector are good. If there are aspects you feel weak in, you may want to develop those sides of yourself. If you find three or more of the key characteristics unappealing, you may want to consider work in a less demanding environment. In the next chapter we will discuss types of questions used by interviewers to rate a candidate's ranking in the seven categories, as well as responses that could help or hinder your chances. Before moving to the next chapter, complete Power Prep Strategy II, which will help strengthen your performance in each key area.

POWER PREP STRATEGY II

Each of the seven key evaluation factors is critical to your interview performance. The following activities will help you clarify your strengths in each area, compensate for your weaknesses, and help you identify the stories that match each area. Your personal trigger stories, like the ones presented in this chapter, can make the difference between your being seen as an average candidate and as an outstanding one.

Factor 1: Aggressiveness and Enthusiasm

What can you do to be an aggressive candidate and how can you demonstrate your aggressiveness in this interview?_____

_____

_____

What genuine enthusiasm do you have for this organization, its products and/or services, and the job itself?_____

_____

_____

What is your best story to demonstrate that you are an aggressive employee?_____

_____

_____

What is your best story to show what you can do when you're enthusiastic about a product or service?_____

_____

_____

Factor 2: Communication Skills

Rate yourself on the following communication skills from 1 to 10, 1 being strongest and 10 weakest:

_____ Listening

_____ Public speaking

_____ Report writing

_____ Letter writing

_____ Creative writing

_____ Debating

_____ Summarizing

_____ Networking

_____ Selling

_____ Negotiating

Next, take the three lowest-rated categories and consider ways to improve them (for example, practice listening or read a book on public speaking).

Item _____Strategy for improvement_____

_____

_____

Item _____Strategy for improvement_____

_____

_____

Item _____Strategy for improvement_____

_____

_____

Factor 3: Record of Success

List the five achievements in your work life of which you are proudest and describe the unique role you played in bringing about a successful outcome.

Achievement 1 _____

Your contribution _____

Achievement 2 _____

Your contribution _____

Achievement 3 _____

Your contribution _____

Achievement 4 _____

Your contribution _____

Achievement 5 _____

Your contribution _____

Factor 4: Rational Thought Process

Which of the following thought processes do you handle well? Assign each item a rating from 1 to 5, 1 being weak, 3 moderate, and 5 strong:

Clarifying problems   1 2 3 4 5

Evaluation alternatives 1 2 3 4 5

Generating solutions   1 2 3 4 5

Testing ideas   1 2 3 4 5

Determining outcomes   1 2 3 4 5

For each of the items you rated 4 or 5, write a brief description of a time when you used that skill effectively. For each of the items you circled 1, 2, or 3, write a way you might strengthen that skill (for example, practice brainstorming or a technique for generating solutions).

Clarifying problems (rating_____) _____

_____

_____

Evaluating alternatives (rating_____) _____

_____

_____

Generating solutions (rating_____) _____

_____

_____

Testing ideas (rating_____) _____

_____

_____

Determining outcomes (rating_____) _____

_____

_____

Factor 5: Maturity

If you were to set your age, not by chronological date, but by level of maturity, how old would you be? _____

If you chose an age older than your actual age, what evidence can you present? If you chose an age younger than your actual age, what can you do to present yourself as more mature than you think you are? List three experiences that address your level of maturity in a positive light.

Work experience _____

Family experience _____

Social experience _____

Factor 6: Planning and Organization

What is the most elaborate project you ever organized? What was your role in the project?

_____

_____

There are many ways to plan; however, there are key components essential to every planning process. Keep the following steps in mind and use them in your interview to show you have an organized mind capable of comprehensive planning. A comprehensive planning process includes:

Mission or purpose. What is it you are trying to achieve?

Goals. What are the long-term targets that will serve your purpose?

Objectives. What specific aims do you have to reach your goals?

Plans/Strategies. What will you do to fulfill your objectives?

Activities. Who is going to implement which parts of the plan, when, and how?

Evaluation. How are you going to judge the success of the venture?

Integrate these six steps of a comprehensive planning process into your presentation of your planning and organizing skills and your interviewer will leave the interview confident in your planning and organizing abilities.

Factor 7: Reaction to Pressure

Interviews are by design stressful situations. Each of us reacts to stress differently. In what ways do your body and your behavior respond to stress? Some frequently reported reactions are sweaty hands, backache, and talking too fast.

A stress reaction can kill an interview. What are the typical things that happen to you when you get nervous and what can you do to compensate?

Examples: Sweaty hands: Arrive early and wash hands.

Talking too fast: Focus on speed of speech and slow down periodically.

Take a moment and list three reactions that your body and behavior have to stress and your strategies to control them.

Reaction 1_____   Strategy_____

Reaction 2_____   Strategy_____

Reaction 3_____   Strategy_____

Interviewers are also looking for evidence that you can handle stress on the job. Describe three incidents from work situations in which you handled stress well.

Incident 1 _____

_____

_____

Incident 2 _____

_____

_____

Incident 3 _____

_____

_____

You've completed a series of exercises that will fine-tune your ability to perform optimally in each of seven key evaluation factors. Review this before your next interview and you will dazzle the interviewer with your competence—and your ability to demonstrate it.

3

Winning Answers to Key Questions

Each of the seven evaluation factors in the previous chapter carries with it some key questions. Your answers to the questions in each category will influence your rating in that category and ultimately your chances in the interview. This chapter presents an overview of the questions that reveal information about a candidate for each category and includes responses and response strategies that can enhance or hinder your chances.

The responses presented for each question are not intended to be a script, but to provide the gist of what a good answer would be. It's important to remember that your responses should match your identity. If your answers ring true you're much more likely to be viewed as a viable candidate.

The questions in this chapter are derived from the audiotape "How Do They Decide" that we developed and is based on thousands of interviews with Fortune 500 recruiters and executives. Each question is analyzed to help the reader understand its significance and the type of information likely to be culled from it. Next, responses are given that are considered by experts to be appropriate (winner answers) or inappropriate (killer answers). Each response will be followed by a critique. Since it is just as important to know what not to say in an interview, we urge you to read and consider the killer answers as well as the winner answers.

CATEGORY 1: AGGRESSIVENESS AND ENTHUSIASM

Successful companies depend on a workforce that is aggressive and enthusiastic. Your energy level and commitment to the task at hand will be measured by your responses in this category, as will your ability to convey a sense of excitement and a willingness to go the extra mile for the company.

Aggressiveness concerns your willingness to apply your skills and talents in an assertive, hard-driving way. Organizations seeking new employees, regardless of rank, role, or area of expertise, want people who believe their own function is critical to the organization and warrants a diligent approach. Similarly, they are looking for people whose enthusiasm for the organization and its products and services is unbridled.

QUESTION 1

Why do you feel you can be successful in this position?

Analysis A fairly open-ended question, this provides an opportunity for applicant to demonstrate a sense of excitement and challenge. The response will give the interviewer key information on applicant's drive and self-confidence in relation to this position.

Killer Answer I don't know; I'm pretty good at most things I do. If I get offered this job and decide to take it I'm sure I could rise to the occasion. I've always been successful in the past.

Critique Although this may on the surface sound acceptable, it is lacking in several ways. First, the language is weak. Phrases such as "I don't know" and "pretty good" do not reflect the sort of aggressiveness required to break into the best companies. Further, lumping this position with everything else the applicant has done dilutes the person's success and real enthusiasm for this particular position. Finally, the suggestion that the applicant might not take the position once offered also reflects a lack of enthusiasm.

Winner Answer Given my history, this is the perfect position at this point in my career. I have been studying this field and watching your organization for several years in anticipation of such an opportunity. I have the requisite skills [tell a brief story to prove it]. I am in a perfect position to take this job and really run with it.

Critique This is a strong response because it tells the interviewer the applicant has both the skill and the knowledge to do the job. The story illustrating the applicant's skill reinforces the initial statement. Finally, the applicant's intention to "run with it" supports the desired enthusiasm and aggressiveness.

QUESTION 2

What is your greatest strength and weakness, and how will these affect your performance here?

Analysis The biggest danger with this question is that it is really two questions in one, plus a follow-up. The two pitfalls are not taking the part about strengths seriously enough, and taking the part about weaknesses too seriously. Remember, your responses will not only inform the interviewer of your assets and liabilities but also present a broad view of your values and your sense of self-worth.

Killer Answer In terms of strengths, I really can't pinpoint one thing that stands out. I think my skills are pretty well rounded. As far as weaknesses go, I guess I get bored if a project drags on too long.

Critique The biggest problem with this response is that the applicant essentially refuses to answer the first part of the question. The response to the second part hints at a potential lack of enthusiasm. Finally, the responses to the first two parts of the question leave the applicant with little chance for a respectable response to the third part.

Winner Answer In terms of strengths, I believe my greatest asset is that I have a highly organized mind, capable of creating order out of confusion. My greatest weakness perhaps is that I have little patience for people who don't value the same sense of order that I do. I believe my organizational skills can help this organization achieve its goals more quickly, and that my appreciation for streamlining complex problems can sometimes rub off on my coworkers.

Critique This response does three important things. It clearly identifies the applicant's greatest strength. It identifies a weakness that really could just as easily be perceived as a strength. Finally, it points out the benefits of the applicant's strength and weakness to the organization and to other employees.

QUESTION 3

Have you ever been put on the spot by a professor or advisor and felt unsure of yourself? How did you respond?

Analysis This question probes applicant's ability to work in unfamiliar territory. It is designed to get a picture of applicant's willingness and ability to tackle assignments that are a stretch beyond current levels of competence.

Killer Answer I believe it's important to question authority. If I learned anything in school it's that a lot of professors think they have all the answers when they're really out of touch with what's happening in the real world. You know, all that ivory tower stuff.

Critique The biggest problem with this response is that it shifts the focus away from the applicant. Serious interviewers are not interested in your opinion of higher education. Rather, they want to know how you handle yourself in the situation presented in the question. The other real problem with this response is that it creates doubts in the interviewer's mind about your willingness to follow instructions.

Winner Answer I tried to make the most of my years in school, so I often took courses in areas I was unfamiliar with. Consequently I was often challenged by my professors. Whenever I found myself in a situation where I knew less than I might about a subject, I tried to anticipate the questions so that I'd be prepared to respond. When challenged I'd try to make as educated a guess as possible, acknowledge what I didn't know, and take it from there. For example [give an illustration if you have one]...

Critique The strongest thing about this response is that it articulates the applicant's willingness to deal with difficult situations. It also shows that the applicant has ambition and a clear sense of how to approach novel and ambiguous problems.

QUESTION 4

Have you ever received a grade lower than you expected? If so, what did you do about it?

Analysis In addition to revealing information about applicant's enthusiasm and aggressiveness, responses to this question reveal information about a sense of fairness and willingness to fight for a cause.

Killer Answer I remember one time I thought I deserved a B and got a C. I went to the instructor and he showed me the breakdown of the grades—I was on the border but clearly in the C category. I was glad I checked it out rather than just accept it at face value.

Critique This answer starts out strong but ends with a dramatic fizzle. It looks as if applicant is committed to following through at first. Then it becomes clear he or she lacks the drive to create change.

Winner Answer I had a horrible experience once with an earth science professor. The man was known for his bias in favor of science majors, which I was not. There was a large group of nonmajors in the class who felt he had unrealistic expectations about our knowledge base. Many of the students did poorly as a result of his bias. While I did okay, I joined the other students in issuing a statement to the department head suggesting there be a review of the way the course was presented.

Critique This response demonstrates applicant's ability to overcome a difficult situation and come out on top. It also indicates a high level of commitment to a sense of fairness. Finally it exhibits applicant's willingness to get involved for the benefit of the group.

QUESTION 5

For job advancement would you consider an advanced degree?

Analysis This is a simple question designed to gauge your ambition and see if your level of investment in your future dictates an investment in you by the company.

Killer Answer I don't know; I've got my B.A. in management and I think I got a pretty good education. I think real world experience is far more valuable than anything you learn in school.

Critique Although this response attempts to show the applicant in a positive light and indirectly to flatter the interviewer (who is part of the "real world"), it speaks poorly of applicant's willingness to improve. Consequently, applicant conveys, at best, a lack of ambition and, at worst, arrogance.

Winner Answer I learned a lot as an undergraduate and would certainly consider an advanced degree for the right reasons. I'd want to be careful though; I think a lot of people go back to school for the wrong reasons. If I found I was doing work I really valued and I needed more education to excel in that area I certainly wouldn't hesitate.

Critique This response shows ambition, enthusiasm, and drive. It also shows that the applicant has a discriminating mind and is careful about making major career decisions.

QUESTION 6

What competitive activities have you participated in? Were they worthwhile?

Analysis This question gets at your comfort with and confidence in competition by probing your history with structured competitive situations. It is a perfect opportunity to discuss any team activities or organized efforts in which competition was a key factor.

Killer Answer I'm a highly competitive person by nature. I think I take a competitive slant on virtually everything I do. After all, that's how you survive in the corporate jungle, isn't it?

Critique Applicant has been doing too much reading about sharks and Huns. Although the corporate world is highly competitive, those involved in it resent the image that they are a bunch of seething barracudas.

Winner Answer I like team sports and participate in them as often as I can. I used to play a lot of basketball and still do when I get a chance. Working with a team toward a common end and outperforming the competition can be really thrilling.

Critique This response suggests that applicant has a healthy view of competition. The implication is that he or she would use competitive energy to outdo the competition, not to undo the work of colleagues.

CATEGORY 2: COMMUNICATION SKILLS

I met a man last week who ran a video production business; I learned that he had a Ph.D. in physics and used to teach at the college level. When he found out that I worked with career changers for a living, he said, "It's easy to change careers these days. All you need is to be able to write well and know how to talk to people." While I'm not sure it's as simple as that, the point that communication skills are crucial to the successful job seeker is valid. Because questions in this category address your ability to communicate, they are the questions most likely to be used to judge your skill in this area. This is the one category in which interviewers get to see the applicants in action, not just hear about their performance. Therefore, it is one of those categories that can make you or break you. Anyone who has done any teaching, training, or sales presentations knows that the more you do it, the better it comes across. That's why we strongly urge you to practice your responses to the 50 questions in this chapter before an interview. There's a good chance that your ability to communicate effectively will have a major impact on the number and types of offers you get. The following questions are designed to determine an applicant's ability to communicate effectively.

QUESTION 7

How do you go about influencing someone to accept your ideas?

Analysis Your answer will tell the interviewer, first, how comfortable you are with the notion of influencing others, and second, how able you are at influencing.

Killer Answer I usually depend on the value of the idea. If it's a good idea and the people I'm dealing with are reasonable, I generally don't have much trouble getting my ideas accepted.

Critique The problem with this response is that it doesn't address the real problem, which is how you deal with people who don't think your idea is good. It suggests that you are willing to work in a harmonious situation, but not in a discordant one.

Winner Answer That's something I've worked very hard on over the years. At some point I realized that good ideas, even great ideas, sometimes don't get accepted. I now appreciate the fact that the way you present an idea is just as important as the idea itself. When trying to influence people I usually try to put myself in their position and think about their perspective. I'm then able to present thoughts to them in a way more likely to succeed.

Critique This answer demonstrates your appreciation of the complexity of interpersonal communication and the difficulty in getting others to change their minds. It conveys an understanding of the importance of strategy when influencing someone and articulates a reasoned approach. Finally, you demonstrate an understanding of the importance of form as well as substance when communicating under difficult circumstances.

QUESTION 8

What experience have you had in making oral presentations? How do you rate your oral presentation skills?

Analysis This question is intended to discern your comfort in public speaking and to gain a self-assessment of your skill.

Killer Answer I think everyone gets nervous making presentations. I can do them, but to tell you the truth, people don't always listen. Sometimes I think it's better just to give people the information on paper and then answer questions.

Critique This answer clearly places you at the bottom of the pool. It not only suggests discomfort with oral presentations but also implies that you don't need develop your oral presentation skills.

Winning Answer I read somewhere that public speaking is the number one fear of people in this country. I figured that if most people are so scared of it, harnessing my own fear and mastering the skill of oral presentation would put me strides ahead of the competition. So I do presentations every chance I get and find that the more I do them the more comfortable I get—and the better I get.

Critique This is a strong response because it comments specifically on your competence in this area and shows that you are working on further developing an important skill. By acknowledging that oral presentations are tricky, the applicant also demonstrates a willingness to be honest and candid.

QUESTION 9

How would you compare your oral skills to your writing skills?

Analysis This is what I call a booby-trapped question. Whenever you get a question that asks you to compare two things, beware. The question is designed to get you to speak about your weaknesses.

Killer Answer [Any response that says why you're better at one skill or the other.]

Critique You took the bait.

Winner Answer It seems organizations are more dependent than ever on the ability of employees to be articulate both orally and in writing. I constantly take advantage of opportunities to develop my oral and written communication skills. These days I think they're vital competencies for anyone expecting to be successful in the business world.

Critique This response avoids the trap of being seen as weak in either area and demonstrates your understanding of the importance of strong communication skills. Most important, it reassures the interviewer that you have a solid base of generic skills that can be drawn on regardless of the direction the organization takes.

QUESTION 10

What do you least like about writing a term paper?

Analysis This question probes your willingness to do research, uncover information, and come up with answers to difficult questions.

Killer Answer The worst thing is when it's on a topic I'm really not interested in. I don't mind doing the research if it's interesting stuff, but so often there is no real world application of the material being researched.

Critique Although many readers may be nodding their heads in agreement with this response, it leaves the interviewer uneasy. Often a job may require tasks that are mundane and tedious. Hearing an applicant state a dislike for anything uninteresting is unsettling.

Winner Answer If I'm doing a good job I'm probably discovering that there is an unlimited amount of information available on a subject. The task I find most difficult is deciding when I've obtained enough data to stop researching and start writing.

Critique This response demonstrates applicant's understanding of and willingness to do research. It shows an ability to uncover in-depth information and suggests that applicant is competent at writing term papers.

QUESTION 11

How should supervisors and subordinates interact?

Analysis This question is designed to discover applicant's approach to communication in the organizational hierarchy. The response is likely to indicate an applicant's level of skill in a potentially complex area.

Killer Answer I like to think that we can be friends. After all if you're going to work closely with someone you might as well get to know that person. That way everyone understands each other and you can avoid a lot of unnecessary conflict.

Critique The worst thing about this response is that it demonstrates a high level of immaturity. Anyone the least bit knowledgeable about relationships in the workplace knows that conflict is an inevitable part of working life. The notion that creating close friendships can simplify things shows a real lack of understanding of the relationship between work and personal boundaries.

Winner Answer I believe that clear communication throughout the hierarchy of an organization is critical to the organization's thriving. I'd like to think I've developed good strong skills in that area. In terms of superior-subordinate relationships I think it's most important to realize that each person and each relationship is different. The best approach for me is to begin with no assumptions and see how the relationship evolves.

Critique This answer indicates an understanding of the complexity of interpersonal communication and the diversity of human relationships. Applicant clearly articulates the importance of strong communication skills and conveys confidence in this area.

QUESTION 12

How would you be described by a close friend?

Analysis This question is designed to shed some light on an applicant's character. It's one of those questions that seems to have nothing to do with an applicant's potential, but it reflects a trend in business for hiring people with high personal standards as well as strong skills.

Killer Answer I think people would say I'm a fun person to be with. The best way to describe me is I like to work hard and play hard.

Critique Although this response may sound entirely positive to some of you, it raises several problems. First, it does not answer the question, leaving the interviewer wondering whether applicant has any close relationships. Also it leaves the interviewer wondering about the nature of "play hard" and raises some potentially damaging questions, for example, concerning drug or alcohol abuse.

Winner Answer My friends are very important to me. The most important aspect of my relationship with them is the sense that we can rely on each other. We're all very busy so there are times we don't meet often. With the few people I would call close friends it's knowing that we're there for each other that counts.

Critique This response reflects a sense of maturity, so much a concern in today's corporate world. Applicant's commitment to high standards and to a few key people suggests that the individual is well balanced. It also rings true. Don't use it if it doesn't—it won't work.

QUESTION 13

How do you get along with coworkers?

Analysis The response to this question, along with previous ones on superior-subordinate relationships and friendships, gives the interviewer an overall impression of your ability to communicate effectively. In a sense it is the most critical of the communication questions because 80 percent of the people who leave their jobs, according to the Department of Labor, do so because they don't fit in with the other people. Your ability to communicate your effectiveness in peer relationships will help ease the interviewer's concern that you may be yet another bad match.

Killer Answer I get along with most everyone. I'm an easygoing kind of person. I've never really met anyone that I couldn't get along with. Once in a while everyone meets someone that they don't like as much as the rest of the staff, but I try to overlook that. If someone is really obnoxious they usually don't last anyway—so I wait it out, knowing that eventually they'll disappear.

Critique Although this response, like some of the other killer answers, seems fairly harmless, it has several problems. First, no one gets along with everyone. After making this broad statement the interviewee then goes on to talk about people that he or she doesn't like, making the response sound somewhat contradictory. Finally, the interviewee breaks the cardinal rule of interviewing—never say negative things about other people.

Winner Answer I generally get along very well with coworkers. Occasionally I might run into a conflict with someone. When that happens I usually focus on what the conflict is about rather than on personalities. I find that approach helps me maintain a respectful relationship with anyone, and often leads to resolution and strengthened relationships.

Critique This response suggests that applicant is well balanced, with a high level of human relations skills. By making the distinction between problems and personalities, applicant appears to be someone who has worked out problems in the past and has a history of successful interpersonal relationships.

CATEGORY 3: RECORD OF SUCCESS

Your record of success is your most important credential for gaining access to the best companies. Effectively conveying a view of yourself as a person with an impressive track record will do more for your chances than any other single tactic. Careful review of the questions in this category will help arm you for your campaign.

There are two tacks you can take, depending on what you have to work with and the job you're applying for. If your background vividly illustrates your ability to do the job in question, you should choose the best examples and present them.

If, however, your record of success has no apparent relationship to the job, your task becomes one of education as well as illustration. If the interviewer has an appreciation for the transferability of skills, all you need is to make the connection between the examples you choose and the job in question. Some interviewers, however, like some applicants, will not see the link between history and potential future. What you must do then is point out how your past relates to what the company needs. By showing that the skills you've used in the past are directly transferable and applicable to the tasks required on the job in question, you allay fears and, if you do it well, effectively plead your case.

QUESTION 14

What do you consider your most significant accomplishment and why?

Analysis This question gives the interviewer insight into your values. What you choose to talk about will reveal much about your standards and priorities.

Killer Answer Just making it through school was tough. You know I worked my way through school. I'm proud of having been able to juggle studies and work at the same time.

Critique On the surface this may seem like a good answer; many of you have probably used it, although it falls short in several ways. First, it is fairly common today for students to work their way through school, so there's nothing unique about it. Second, it's too general, focusing on an ongoing process rather than a specific activity that highlights your uniqueness.

Winner Answer [Rather than give you a specific line of thought to work with, I suggest you need to think of something you've done that highlights your uniqueness. Some examples: Won first prize in a math competition, was elected class officer, managed a family crisis, wrote a comprehensive school newspaper article, won a debating contest, rebuilt a car engine from scratch, reorganized a department, successfully launched a new product line.]

Critique Each of these examples is unique, impressive, and likely to set you apart from the crowd. Remember that you don't necessarily need to have received formal recognition for your accomplishment. It has to be something you did extremely well and are proud of. Spend some time thinking about this. It will work much better for you than a generic "worked my way through school" response.

QUESTION 15

Under what conditions have you been most successful in your undertakings?

Analysis This question probes the conditions under which you work best. Your response will reveal information about your preferred way of working, factors that influence your chances of success, and possibly your limitations.

Killer Answer I can succeed at just about anything I put my mind to. As long as I know what's expected of me, I usually get results.

Critique Although this seems like a reasonable response, it has flaws. As with the previous question, it is what we would call a generic response that leaves a weak impression at best. The real problem with this answer is that it presumes the organization is looking for people who are good at following others' directions, not charting their own. In these lean times, most corporations are seeking people who are self-motivated. Communicating that you are someone who needs direction from others can be deadly.

Winner Answer My approach to problem solving involves a systematic process of gathering relevant information about a problem, clearly identifying the problem, setting a strategy, and then implementing it. I find most people skip the first two parts and jump straight to strategy. As long as I have enough information and a clear view of the problem, I can tackle anything.

Critique This response demonstrates that applicant has solved difficult problems in the past, has thought about strategy, and has developed a method for solving difficult problems. It also shows a sense of confidence and willingness to use proven skills in the future.

QUESTION 16

How hard do you work to achieve your objectives?

Analysis The most obvious thing about this question is that the interviewer wants to hear that applicant is a hard worker. The key is presenting a response that shows applicant's willingness and ability to fulfill responsibilities.

Killer Answer My energy level on a particular task depends on the difficulty of the task and how badly I want to achieve it. If I decide that something is really important I'll put my all into it and make it happen.

Critique The first mistake here is the introduction of the idea that applicant has a limited reservoir of energy. No successful company is interested in anyone who doesn't seem to have unbounded energy. Second, the notion that the applicant works hard only on tasks that he or she is personally committed to suggests an unwillingness to accept less than desirable assignments.

Winner Answer For me the question is not how hard I work. It's a given that if I've set an objective or if I've been given an important assignment I work as hard as necessary to achieve the desired results. The question for me is how smart do I work—that is, what can I do to make the completion of the task come as easily and smoothly as possible so I can move on to other things?

Critique The strength of this response is that it suggests that applicant has unlimited energy and a high level of commitment. It also indicates that applicant approaches problems so as to ensure maximum utilization of his or her resources—what the question was really after.

QUESTION 17

Has competition had any positive or negative impact on your accomplishments? How?

Analysis The question is designed to weed out candidates who are uncomfortable in a competitive environment. The interviewer is looking for the extent to which applicant feels intimidated by competitive situations.

Killer Answer I like competition. It sometimes gives me the push I need to get going. I never find it overwhelming. It's just a part of life and part of what keeps me going.

Critique Most people will not believe this response for one minute. Also, it seems to patronize. Most people find competition overwhelming at least some of the time. The response also hints at a lack of motivation and the need for competition as a motivating agent.

Winner Answer If I was afraid of competition I wouldn't be applying for a job in a place like this. I know competition is built in. The most important thing to me is knowing the competition and being clear about what it is we're competing for. When I'm in a competitive situation I like to make sure I understand what's at stake. Once I understand the game plan, I wholeheartedly enjoy competing.

Critique This response communicates the same positive outlook on competition as the killer answer, but without the whitewash. It demonstrates that applicant has a clearly defined way of dealing with competition based on prior experience.

QUESTION 18

What do you consider your earning potential to be five years from now?

Analysis The real meaning behind this question is "Are you ambitious enough for us and do you have far-reaching goals for yourself?"

Killer Answer I'd like to be making $100,000 a year. There are lots of things I want: a nice car, my own house, maybe a boat. I think a hundred grand five years from now would be a good start.

Critique No comment.

Winner Answer I believe my talents can earn me a decent living; that's why I'm applying to a prestigious company such as yours. I plan to make enough money to live comfortably and am willing to do what it takes to ensure that I am well paid throughout my career.

Critique Unlike the previous answer, this applicant has the good sense not to talk in dollar amounts. Unless you're in salary negotiation, naming numbers is highly inappropriate, not to mention tacky. Showing a sense of self-respect gives the interviewer confidence in your value as an applicant.

CATEGORY 4: RATIONAL THOUGHT PROCESS

We know a man who was a supervisor at a paper production company. He lost his job when it was discovered that one of the machines he was responsible for had cut seven hours' worth of 8½ x 11 paper as 8 x 11½. What cost him his job was not his mistake, but the fact that the machine had been retooled that morning. The sensible thing for anyone with his responsibility would be to double-check the settings to make sure the measurements were accurate.

Stories like this have made interviewers pay so much attention to rational thought process. Rational thought process refers to the capability and tendency for a person to think and act in a lucid, careful, and somewhat predictable fashion. The more clear, succinct, and mindful of detail a person seems in an interview, the more likely that the person will score well in this category. Although there is no guarantee that rational behavior will follow a display of rational thought process, the interviewer will most likely make judgments in this area based on your response.

Rational thought process is one of those categories that could make the difference in a close interview. If two equally qualified candidates give acceptable performances in an interview the job would probably go to the one who seemed most succinct and rational. To the interviewer a rational thought process translates to a higher level of productivity, and fewer mistakes on the job.

QUESTION 19

What are the most important features you are looking for in a job and why?

Analysis This challenges your rational thought process by presenting an open-ended inquiry into your priorities. As important as your response to this question is your ability to demonstrate an understanding of what a good job might be.

Killer Answer I want a job that will really showcase my talents, one with high visibility. I like to think that working in a company like yours will set me apart from the crowd.

Critique Aside from portraying applicant as an egomaniac with a high need for recognition, this response has other problems. The problem is that it does not address the needs of the employer—something every response should do. In addition it leaves the interviewer wondering if applicant has any understanding of the nature of work.

Winner Answer I'm looking for a job that utilizes my strongest skills, such as [name specific skills]. I think it's also important that my role in the organization be clearly tied to the goals of the organization. It would also be great to have a job that is at times challenging, one that stretches me beyond my current abilities.

Critique Although fairly brief, this response accomplishes three things: it highlights applicant's skills, demonstrates an understanding of the need for relevance in one's job, and shows understanding of the importance of change and development.

QUESTION 20

How do you think our company determines success?

Analysis This question is designed to see what, if anything, the applicant knows about the company. It's meant to weed out those not interested enough or not smart enough to do their homework.

Killer Answer Well, because you're a highly successful company I imagine you're concerned with staying on top and beating the competition. I'll bet you consider bottom-line results as your key measure of success.

Critique Although this response may be true, it is too general to have a positive impact. It tells the interviewer nothing of applicant's interest in and knowledge of the company. A fair assumption would be that applicant knows nothing about this organization and its goals.

Winner Answer I've watched your company introduce a series of new products over the past two years. It seems you take a comprehensive approach to product development and marketing strategy. I think you would measure success by the extent to which new products become front-runners in their market niche.

Critique Although this response (for the sake of illustration) is not much more specific than the killer answer, it shows that applicant has some understanding of what the company does. The suggestion that being number one is important to this organization and is something it has achieved in the past shows a high regard for the organization and its definition of success.

QUESTION 21

What is the most intellectually challenging thing you are looking for in a job and why?

Analysis This question probes applicant's understanding of the need to think critically. The response will give the interviewer a glimpse of applicant's problem-solving capacity.

Killer Answer I'm looking for a job that lets me use what I know. When you go to a good school like I did you learn a lot about the way things should work. It would be great to be able to apply some of that knowledge to a work situation.

Critique Here applicant misses the point and confuses intellectual challenge with prior learning. The response suggests that the applicant has the answers rather than the capacity to formulate new answers to unique problems.

Winner Answer I think it's important to be involved in the short- and long-range planning in the organization. I'd like to think that wherever I ended up in a company I could be involved in some way with its research and development activities. Knowing and being part of where an organization is going is the most intellectually challenging aspect of work for me.

Critique This response indicates that applicant values intellectual challenge and the stretching of personal limits. It also suggests that applicant is motivated toward learning about the organization's future and making a contribution to its endeavors.

QUESTION 22

What is the most intellectually challenging thing you have done?

Analysis This question probes applicant's level of intelligence. It provides the interviewer with a glimpse of the potential problem-solving ability of the applicant.

Killer Answer Well, that's a tough question. I'm not really an intellectual. I'm more of a hands-on kind of person. I mean, what's the point of intellectualizing? I leave that to the professors at the university. I'm more interested in making things happen.

Critique At this point we'd like to introduce the "flake factor." The killer answer is a perfect illustration. In fact, in terms of the flake factor this response is off the charts. Applicant not only berates the interviewer by belittling the question, but shows a decided inability to think at a high level.

Winner Answer A couple of summers ago I worked in an insurance company that was switching over to a computerized mail system. I was only summer help, but I was able, because of some of my computer coursework, to help debug the system. It was really exciting because I was learning as I was doing, but in the long run I was able to suggest some changes that were implemented.

Critique The strength of this response is that it illustrates applicant's ability to take prior learning, apply it to a new situation, learn from experience, and apply the new learning.

QUESTION 23

How did you determine your career choice?

Analysis This question is designed to see whether applicant's choice in pursuing this line of work in this company has any historical origin. Does applicant have a career plan or is he or she aimlessly applying for a variety of jobs?

Killer Answer I've always wanted to work in the corporate world. Ever since I was a kid I've dreamed about becoming at least a vice-president in a large company.

Critique Aside from being hard to believe, this question raises another problem. It suggests that the applicant will be unhappy with anything less than a vice-presidency.

Winner Answer The summer before my senior year I decided it was time to focus on a specific direction. Even though I was a business major I wasn't sure which business I would end up in. I spent some time thinking about my goals, what I was good at, and what I really wanted out of work, and I decided that this industry was my best bet.

Critique This shows applicant has done some serious planning, has narrowed his or her focus, and has targeted a direction. The answer shows an understanding of the importance of personal career planning and demonstrates an ability to make careful personal decisions.

QUESTION 24

What do you consider most valuable, a high salary or job recognition and advancement?

Analysis Here we have the comparison trap again. If you follow the questioner's lead, you lose. Either you choose money over advancement, which is considered tacky and shortsighted, or you run the risk of being viewed as insincere about indifference to money.

Killer Answer Money's not that important to me. What I want is to make a contribution to my company and to reap the more significant rewards of recognition and advancement.

Critique This response smacks of insincerity; even worse, it brings into question applicant's judgment. If money is not all that important, why is applicant seeking work in the corporate world, which by definition must be financially motivated? People not interested in money would probably seek work in environments where the money factor is less central.

Winner Answer For me, those things are inseparable. Although I am not obsessive about money, I assume that with success and the advancement and recognition it brings will come greater financial rewards.

Critique This response is honest and to the point without being in poor taste. It reflects the applicant's ambition and the logical consequences of his or her success.

QUESTION 25

Organize your ladder of success and explain this progression.

Analysis The response will reveal applicant's understanding of how the corporate world operates and the extent to which applicant's expectations are realistic. The response also indicates something about applicant's goals and ambitions.

Killer Answer I'm on the fast track. I'm one of those people who believes that in America hard work pays. I believe that if I choose the right company I can move up the corporate ladder pretty quickly, and ultimately be one of the people running the company. In a first-rate company like this one, that would be success.

Critique Although this response may at first seem reasonable, it has several problems. It echoes the beliefs of many people in the corporate world, but it does not acknowledge the fact that the way things work is changing. The last sentence is a bit too patronizing. To the astute interviewer this response might sound like Horatio Alger.

Winner Answer I think that's probably the biggest challenge facing everyone in the career marketplace today. I think companies are changing the way they deal with career ladders in a dramatic way. Consequently, I think people have to do the same. The key, I think, is finding an organization that can utilize my skills to the fullest extent. Once I find that, I'll do all I can to increase my value to the company. If I'm making an important contribution I believe that career advancement will result.

Critique This demonstrates applicant's understanding of the changing workplace. It reflects an understanding of the problems companies face in relation to individual productivity. It suggests that applicant sees personal career development as tied to performance, and it indicates a drive to succeed without any accompanying unrealistic expectations. Finally, it suggests that the employment contract is one entered into in good faith by employer and employee.

QUESTION 26

What qualities would be most important in determining whom *you* would hire for this position?

Analysis By turning the tables on applicant, this question probes his or her understanding of the needs and requirements of the position. It tells the interviewer the extent to which applicant understands the demands of the position and the priorities of the organization.

Killer Answer I would hire someone like me! I'm hard-working, intelligent, and motivated. That's what you need in a position like this—someone who's really hungry.

Critique In this response applicant fails to take the interviewer's challenge and move beyond the focus on himself or herself. The result is a decided inability to see the overall picture. The response also makes applicant seem desperate for work—a serious disadvantage.

Winner Answer I think the 21st century offer some real challenges for corporations. If I were doing the hiring, regardless of the position, I would look for several things. I'd want somebody who wasn't afraid to make decisions, yet was a team player. I'd want someone who appreciated the implications of global competition, yet wasn't intimidated by a world market. Finally, I'd want someone who realized that quality and service are the keys to a company's success.

Critique In a brief yet direct way the applicant demonstrates an ability to see and understand the employer's needs. By focusing on teamwork, decision making, the world market, quality, and service, the applicant presents a clear view of the priorities of many in the corporate world facing the 21st century.

QUESTION 27

What are some of the most creative things you have done?

Analysis In addition to probing for examples of creativity, the question also investigates what aspects of creativity applicant most values.

Killer Answer When I was in high school I had a pretty big role in a class play. Actually I did a lot of acting in high school. I'd say that was my most creative period.

Critique Here applicant makes the classic mistake of equating the word *creativity* with traditional creative activities. Unfortunately, most interviewers see little applicable relationship between creative endeavors and creative problem solving on the job.

Winner Answer One of my most creative periods was when I helped a friend run for student union president at college. Essentially I was responsible for running her campaign, which meant creating a platform on which to run, developing strategies for campaigning, and coming up with ways to increase our support base. For example, one thing we did was run free coffeehouses, where students could hear good music and find out about our positions. It was a very creative period in my life because we were constantly trying to find new angles to pursue.

Critique The strength of this response lies in its application of creative skills to a complex situation. The applicant portrays the ability to approach a multifaceted task in a creative, problem-solving way. By giving a specific example, applicant demonstrates a capacity to be a creative problem solver.

QUESTION 28

Do you agree that grade-point average is an indication of how successful you would be in this company?

Analysis This question has two purposes. If applicant did well in school the interviewer is searching for an understanding that workplace success is different from academic success. If applicant did poorly in school the interviewer is looking to see if this indicates a problem with the individual's problem-solving capacity.

Killer Answer (for someone with poor grades) I don't know, look at Dan Quayle, he certainly did okay for himself—and with a C average. I don't think grades mean that much.

Killer Answer (for someone with good grades) Yes, I think if you can make it in a tough school as I did, it's an indication that you can succeed in the workplace.

Critique The first response is clearly meant to be distracting and is totally inappropriate. It also brings politics into the process, which can backfire.

The second response shows arrogance and suggests a lack of understanding of the difference between academic and workplace problems.

Winner Answer (for someone with poor grades) I think it's important to show the capacity to get good grades. If a person has a poor track record in every subject it might make me nervous. However, not everyone is going to be committed to excelling in every subject. The important thing from my perspective is that there be some highlights in an individual's academic career that point to potential.

Winner Answer (for someone with good grades) While managing an academic career is less complex than a demanding job, I believe there is a correlation. To me the most important thing about a strong academic record is that it reflects a commitment to excellence.

Critique Both responses frame the person's situation positively: the first by pointing out that there was some successful academic work, the second by pointing to the commitment to excellence. Both responses effectively speak in the third person, thus removing the danger of seeming too apologetic or arrogant.

QUESTION 29

If you could construct your own job within our organization, what factors would you include?

Analysis This question is aimed at applicant's understanding of the complexity of the contemporary workplace. Its intent is to understand applicant's appreciation for the need to hire people who can make a range of contributions.

Killer Answer The most important thing to me is making sure that my role is clear and that expectations are realistic. Too many people get burned, I think, when one day they find out they're not as valued as they thought they were.

Critique This response paints a picture of a fearful employee, looking over his or her shoulder while waiting for the ax to fall. It does little to convey applicant's understanding of the importance of having employees who can meet diverse organizational needs.

Winner Answer First, I'd want it to be a job that could use my strongest skills, specifically [mention specific skills]. I'd also want it to be a judgment job, one that was really necessary to meet the goals of the organization. Ideally it would also be one that allowed for some growth and diversification in the future.

Critique This response demonstrates the applicant's understanding that a good match involves hiring someone whose skills are needed, whose function is clear, and whose potential is great. It leaves the interviewer with a sense that applicant would make a rich contribution if chosen.

CATEGORY 5: MATURITY

As organizations struggle to find the most responsible and conscientious employees, the need for applicants to demonstrate a high level of maturity becomes crucial. The applicant needs to keep in mind that interviewers are looking for mature, highly developed individuals. Here maturity implies a perspective that tolerates the ambiguity and uncertainty that anyone with major responsibility faces at work. Applicants confronted with the maturity issue must be able to convey their capacity to think and act responsibly. The key is to convince the interviewer of your ability to see the whole picture and make judgments that reflect sound thinking.

QUESTION 30

In what ways have you been a leader?

Analysis Leadership potential is one of the most highly valued traits in the corporate world. Your response to this question can go a long way in the campaign for a job offer.

Killer Answer Some people are born leaders and I think I'm one of them. I don't think leadership is a quality you can teach. Either you have it or you don't.

Critique Aside from raising the fatal swelled head again, this response falls short in other ways. It does not say anything substantive about applicant, and it implies that this person would not contribute to the leadership potential of other people in the organization.

Winner Answer I've had several jobs where I've played a leadership role, responsible for seeing that jobs get done, and I've always had successful outcomes. More important though, I feel in the past few years that I've developed an ability to spot potential in others and have been able to foster their development. For me, that's the real challenge of leadership: helping others meet their potential.

Critique This indicates that you have a successful track record (adding an illustration would strengthen it). More important, it shows that you have an understanding of what the outcome of effective leadership can be, thus suggesting that you are speaking from experience.

QUESTION 31

In your adult life what accomplishment has given you the most satisfaction?

Analysis The response will give the interviewer a quick insight into your personal values and standards. What you choose to speak about will create an immediate impression of what you hold in high esteem.

Killer Answer In my last job I managed to save enough money— from bonuses and some investments—to get the car of my dreams. I consider that a great accomplishment.

Critique Aside from showing the candidate's ability to manage personal finances, this response does little to illustrate the candidate's maturity. On the contrary, by focusing on the fulfillment of a personal interest, the candidate fails to emphasize career aspirations.

Winner Answer In my last job I took over my boss's responsibilities for two months while he was ill. Although I was relatively new on the job, I was able to pick up the additional responsibilities and effectively meet the demands of both positions. It felt really satisfying to be able to respond to a crisis like that and deliver.

Critique The strength of this response is that it relates a unique accomplishment, emphasizes applicant's commitment and diligence, and suggests formidable competence. By addressing the nature of his or her satisfaction, applicant paints a picture of a highly desirable candidate—one willing and able to perform at an unusually high level.

QUESTION 32

What determines your personal choices, and would you agree that others should use the same criteria?

Analysis One sign of maturity is developing a way of making sense of the world. This question probes the extent to which you have established a way of making choices that reflects your maturity.

Killer Answer I like to take things as they come. I find that I can handle almost any situation if I have to. I don't really have a set of criteria; I just do what the situation demands. Besides, I don't think I can dictate to other people how they should handle things. I believe in everyone's individuality.

Critique This response comes directly out of the "here and now, do your own thing" mentality of the 1960s and 1970s and will leave you at the unemployment office until the next fad comes and goes. To the potential employer this attitude reflects a lack of commitment and willingness to take a stand—both characteristics the employer of the 1990s wants dearly.

Winner Answer It seems to me that the real challenge in today's fast-paced work world is maintaining a sense of balance. That way I'm sure to make choices that keep me feeling my best and most productive. I think a sense of balance is important for everyone interested in functioning at the highest level.

Critique The most important thing about this response is that it shows that you have thought about decision making and have developed an approach that works. In addition, the implication that you can handle the demands of a highly competitive job is comforting to any employer taking on the responsibility of a potential employee's health care.

QUESTION 33

What would you do differently if you were to start college again?

Analysis This question is designed to see if applicant—particularly the recent graduate—has made the transition from student to adult in the way he or she thinks about learning.

Killer Answer I don't think I'd change a thing. Those college years were wonderful years. Sometimes I wish I could replay them. You know, I really got a lot out of school.

Critique This response suggests that applicant is still fighting adulthood, pining for the simpler, less responsible school days. It would send shivers up an interviewer's spine.

Winner Answer I think if I were to start school again I would be less intimidated by the process. I would challenge my professors more; and I would use what I've learned about the system to make it work more to my advantage, to ensure that I got the most from the experience.

Critique This response shows that applicant has demystified the college experience and has developed a critical eye for analyzing experiences and systems. It also suggests that applicant has high standards and is committed to high-quality learning.

QUESTION 34

What have been your greatest disappointments and how did you respond?

Analysis Like the previous question, this goes directly to the maturity issue. It reveals information about applicant's standards, values, and priorities.

Killer Answer When I first started working after I got out of school I was shocked at the expectations of most employers. The idea of spending 60 to 70 hours a week at work was a real shock. I believe that if you're really good you can do any job in no more than 45 to 50 hours a week.

Critique Although the amount of time people are expected to work is an issue many professionals are concerned about, the last thing an employer wants to hear is that you set specific restrictions on your time. In addition, choosing to respond to this question by complaining about employers' demands shows a lack of maturity.

Winner Answer When I first got out of school I initially thought I would find a job and an organization that would last a lifetime. Once I got into the market I realized that finding the right job in the right company might take a while. Now that I understand the way the job market works a little better, I can handle it. The good jobs may take a little longer to find but in the long run I think it pays to be careful.

Critique This response shows that applicant's priority is career stability. By emphasizing the quality of the work situation as a key concern, applicant projects a sense of maturity and depth of understanding of the world of work. The response also suggests that applicant can handle uncertainty—an important survival skill.

QUESTION 35

What are the most important rewards you expect from a job?

Analysis Again, what you choose to talk about reflects your level of maturity as much as the position you take. Also important here is to remember the "no money talk" rule. Unless you're in negotiation, avoid talking about money.

Killer Answer I want to work for an organization that recognizes quality and isn't afraid to reward a job well done. Since I expect to outperform my peers I would expect appropriate remuneration for my accomplishments.

Critique Once again the problem of egos arises. In this response the person conveys a sense of inappropriate superiority and raises a red flag to the interviewer that says "difficult person."

Winner Answer What's most important to me is that the job I take is a good match. By that I mean it will allow me to do what I do well—thus giving me a sense of satisfaction. I also want a job that demands that I stretch myself beyond my current level, forcing me to develop myself.

Critique This double-barreled response—satisfaction from a job well done and the stretching of personal limits for growth—will leave the interviewer eating out of the palm of your hand.

QUESTION 36

Under what circumstances have your associates relied on you?

Analysis One of the ways employers measure maturity is by assessing how much an applicant demonstrates an ability to work with others. This question is targeted toward measuring applicant's ability to engender trust from others and to work cooperatively.

Killer Answer That happens all the time. Once people realize I'm good at what I do they rely on me to do it. That's really not a problem for me.

Critique Anytime someone says, "That's really not a problem for me," there's probably a problem. This is especially true when no suggestion has been made that a problem exists. The other problem is that the answer is so vague and generalized, it lacks authenticity. The interviewer is left wondering if applicant has a real problem with relationships or merely doesn't understand the importance of the question. In either case, a lack of depth or maturity would be the concern.

Winner Answer I've often tried to look at the people I work with as a team. I think it makes sense in a competitive environment. Consequently I've often relied on coworkers and encouraged them to rely on me. For example, when I'm working on a particular project with someone, I like to look at the strengths each of us brings to the project and then delineate roles based on our expertise. It usually works out pretty well.

Critique This response suggests that applicant knows how to create cooperative working relationships and has been successful in the past in gaining others' confidence. This response could be made even stronger by illustration—giving an example of an actual project in which applicant created the sort of expertise sharing mentioned in the response.

QUESTION 37

What do you feel it takes to be a professional?

Analysis This question tells the interviewer how well you are established in the working world. It also tells the interviewer the extent to which you think of yourself as a serious, career-minded person rather than just another job hunter.

Killer Answer You've got to be really good at what you do. Once you achieve excellence in whatever it is you do and show it, then people treat you like a professional. I think it takes time and lots of work but eventually it's worth it.

Critique Here the interviewee presents a view of professionalism as something to be obtained, not something good employees (or prospective employees) already possess. By talking about other people's views (that is, being treated like a professional), applicant suggests that professionalism is in the eye of the beholder—not in the actions of the employee.

Winner Answer To me, being a professional means that for any task I take on I do what needs to be done to achieve results. More than that, it means taking responsibility for my performance. Being a professional means most of all being my own taskmaster—in charge, you might say, of my own quality control.

Critique The greatest strength of this response is its language. By using such phrases as "achieve results," "responsibility for my performance," and "my own quality control," it suggests someone who delivers, needs little supervision, and understands the importance of self-motivation.

CATEGORY 6: PLANNING AND ORGANIZATION

In searching for strong candidates, organizational leaders know that they need people who can tolerate change and flux. The two key skills interviewers are searching for in this section are the ability to plan and the ability to organize.

When seeking an understanding of a person's ability to plan, interviewers are looking for applicant's understanding of the impact of the past on the present and the ability to use prior and current experience to create plans for the future.

As for applicant's organizing ability, interviewers are looking for a sense of order, sequence, and ability to see the whole picture.

This is a difficult category because the two areas of focus are somewhat general. Therefore, it is important that your presentation be as specific and detailed as possible. When responding to questions about planning, responses that demonstrate one's planning skills in action are most effective. When responding to questions about organizing ability, responses presented in an organized, sequential manner are most effective.

QUESTION 38

How did you prepare for this interview?

Analysis This question addresses applicant's ability to plan by focusing on the thing that applicant and interviewer have in common, the interview. It is an excellent opportunity to demonstrate your ability to plan and organize information.

Killer Answer Well, I really didn't have to plan much. You see, I've been preparing myself to work in a high-powered company for a long time. This feels like a very natural move for me, so I just spent a little time thinking about whether this was the right company for me and figured I'd give it a shot.

Critique This response, besides reflecting a lack of planning ability, assumes that the interviewer values spontaneity. What applicant doesn't realize is that the question is a litmus test for applicant's project management skills.

Winner Answer The first thing I did was study your annual report. I then reviewed the major trade journals for articles on your company to see if there were major projects that would shed light on the company. Then I called people I knew who had recently had some contact with you to find out what their impressions were. While doing all this I took some notes and reviewed them before coming in.

Critique This response shows a clear, organized mind at work. It reflects ability to tackle a problem and generate the kind of data needed.

QUESTION 39

What are your personal long-term and short-term goals? How did you determine them? How did you prepare to meet them, in the long run and the short run?

Analysis This is a difficult question because it is really a four-part statement requiring a multitude of responses. It is important to remember with this set of questions—and they are often presented as a set—that you are being asked about personal goals, not professional ones. This is important because chances are you will be asked separately about professional aspirations, and if you don't distinguish between the two you are left with the less than impressive task of having to repeat yourself. The question is in the planning and organizing section because it sheds light on your ability to use these skills in your personal life.

Killer Answer I read somewhere that my generation will be the first one in American history to be worse off than the previous generation. That concerns me and my goal is to make sure I don't come up short in the long run. That may sound pessimistic but I'm a realist and I believe it's important to face facts.

Critique Aside from focusing on the negative condition of the economy—an unwise move—this response is deficient for several reasons. First, it attempts to lump all the questions into one. Second, it is too philosophical, thus revealing nothing about planning or organizing. Finally, it suggests that applicant has a less than optimistic view of his or her future and is primarily concerned with overcoming obstacles and surviving—not thriving.

Winner Answer Like any realistic goals, mine change periodically. My personal strategy, both long- and short-term, is to keep assessing where I am in relation to a current goal and modifying my plans accordingly. For example, every five years I establish a personal plan with an overall goal and set of objectives. I review my progress every six months and make the necessary modifications. My current plan obviously includes a career shift toward more satisfying work. Aside from that, I'm meeting the personal goals I've set most recently.

Critique This response shows an organized mind, one adept at planning. By discussing your approach to personal goal setting, you convey a sense of self-esteem and confidence in your ability to manage personal affairs.

QUESTION 40

What is your personal and professional five-year goal?

Analysis This question continues to probe your ability to plan, and it lets the interviewer know the extent to which your goals match what the company can do for you.

Killer Answer I like to play it one day at a time. With the way companies change hands today, I think it's ridiculous to do too much personal planning, don't you?

Critique This one belongs in the flake hall of fame. First, the popular "one day at a time" does not work when someone wants insight into your goals. Raising the undoubtedly uncomfortable notion that the company is vulnerable to raiders is also inappropriate. Finally, degrading the question by implying that planning is ridiculous and turning the question back to the interviewer would be the final nail in applicant's coffin.

Winner Answer Five years from now I'd like to have been in a good position for a few years, perhaps even have moved up once, and be looking for another step, either up or laterally within an organization. Personally, I'd like to think I can find an organization I can stay with for a while—one interested in making a mutual investment.

Critique Without being overly specific (and possibly creating limits), this response shows you are ambitious and thoughtful about ways to get established in the organization. By talking about lateral shifts as well as upward moves, you offer a view of yourself as flexible.

QUESTION 41

How would you go about creating a plan for your unit or department if you were in charge?

Analysis This question directly challenges applicant's skill in organizational planning. The response will demonstrate applicant's ability to take an open-ended situation and create a strategic plan.

Killer Answer I guess I'd get everybody together, figure out what we needed to accomplish, set some goals and objectives, and then make it happen.

Critique This answer suggests that applicant knows little about strategic planning other than the need to set goals. It leaves the interviewer wondering if applicant has the competence and confidence to lead.

Winner Answer I believe that planning is one of the most critical skills a manager can have. The key is using a systematic process. First, you need to gather input from all staff members. Next you need to review and analyze the input. Once you understand what you're working with, you create a plan with goals and objectives. Next you implement the plan. Finally, you evaluate, on an ongoing basis, how things are going and adjust as required.

Critique This response shows that applicant is familiar and comfortable with the planning process. This systematic presentation of steps suggests that applicant has done it before and is prepared to do it again.

QUESTION 42

What is your long-term occupational goal?

Analysis Your answer will reveal a great deal about your attitude toward planning and your ability to think at long range. It will give the interviewer insight into your method of planning. It will also provide information about your potential match with the organization.

Killer Answer I think everybody's looking for the same thing. You want to be successful, move up the corporate ladder, and eventually become head honcho. Or if that's not possible, at least become one of the key players.

Critique Any impact this response might have is diluted by the suggestion that everybody wants the same thing. The response essentially says nothing about applicant as an individual, except that he or she has blind ambition. Although there is an attempt in the end to back off, the damage is done, and the interviewer is left with a very vague impression of applicant's plans.

Winner Answer I'd like to think I could function in a leadership role in a solid organization. I've had a strong track record so far, and I believe I've got what it takes to make a significant contribution. My aim is eventually to be responsible for large numbers of projects and people.

Critique Although this response is somewhat open-ended it is specific enough to convey a sense of vision toward the future. Applicant uses the question as an opportunity to suggest that he or she has been a winner in the past and intends to continue winning.

QUESTION 43

How important are details to you?

Analysis Your answer will tell the interviewer how careful you are. It will reveal information about your sense of quality and your willingness and ability to do a thorough job.

Killer Answer I think details are important when they influence the outcome of a situation. Sometimes I think people spend too much time on details and it slows them down, preventing them from finishing their work, and that's unfortunate. I think some people don't know when to move on.

Critique The biggest problem with this response is that it borders on complaint. Applicant is disparaging people who pay much attention to detail. What applicant doesn't realize is that in a competitive environment it's often keen attention to detail that sets a company apart.

Winner Answer I think that attention to detail can make the difference between acceptable results and excellent results. Building in quality controls from the start of a project is, I believe, a way to ensure that the project has the best possible outcome. I believe the more careful you are in the early stages of a project, the less likely you are to have problems in the later stages.

Critique This response assures the interviewer that applicant appreciates the need for quality control. It also demonstrates an understanding of the planning process and shows that applicant has done some thinking about, and perhaps had some success with, planning and organizing projects in the past.

QUESTION 44

How would you change your planning for the future if you could?

Analysis This will reveal how much insight applicant has into the consequences of planning. It will tell the interviewer how well applicant learns from past experience and applies that learning to new situations.

Killer Answer I wouldn't change a thing. Everything has gone so well for me that I'm sure if I keep using my best judgment I'll continue to be happy.

Critique This response shows a decided lack of insight and inability to assess one's own actions critically. It also demonstrates a significant lack of depth in applicant's understanding of the complexity of individual career development.

Winner Answer I think that when people are just starting their careers they tend to assume they know what they want. If I could change anything it would be the care with which I made early decisions, like what to major in, summer jobs, early career decisions, that sort of thing.

Critique This response shows that applicant can do serious self-assessment. By acknowledging that some early decisions could have been handled differently, applicant shows a willingness to learn from mistakes and critically assess and modify behavior to improve performance.

CATEGORY 7: REACTION TO PRESSURE

Ask about the stability of the contemporary U.S. corporation and you will be told that one thing is constant: change. The ability to adapt to and thrive on change is considered a key characteristic of any applicant approaching the corporate arena. Demonstrated ability to respond effectively to pressure is a skill coveted by those choosing new employees for their organizations. Because of the constant pressure that comes with uncertainty, employers are increasingly looking for people who can function well when what's around the corner is a mystery. Your ability to respond positively to questions that shed light on your reactions to pressure and change will greatly enhance your chances. Interviewers know that some people react to stress negatively and become paralyzed, while others react positively and become motivated. Being seen as someone who is motivated rather than paralyzed will take you far in the interview process.

QUESTION 45

If you were selling a product and had a customer who was complaining about poor service, what would you do?

Analysis This question probes applicant's ability to respond to and handle difficult people. The interviewer is looking for a response that suggests that applicant is not easily intimidated.

Killer Answer I believe in the age-old adage, "The customer is always right." I would make sure that the customer left feeling fully satisfied with the product.

Critique Age-old is right! The interviewer probably heard this one from his or her grandfather. Don't insult interviewers by feeding them pap. Remember, the interviewer probably has an IQ equal to or greater than yours.

Winner Answer I would explain that this company prides itself on quality goods and quality service. I would then assure the customer that I will do everything in my power to remedy the situation. Next, I would listen to the complaint, track the problem to its source, and make whatever changes are necessary to satisfy the customer.

Critique This response goes beyond the cliché of the killer answer and shows applicant's commitment to quality service. It indicates that applicant is not intimidated by problems and will do what is necessary to resolve them.

QUESTION 46

What kinds of situations really get you down?

Analysis This question is meant to discover your Achilles' heel. It will tell the interviewer what sorts of stress and pressure cause you to lose perspective, motivation, and performance ability.

Killer Answer I don't get down too often. I'm pretty resilient. What slows me down is having to deal with other people's down times.

Critique Although respondent's instincts are right in not naming a true Achilles' heel (you never want to do that in an interview), denying any potential obstacles leaves the interviewer suspicious. Applicant also breaks the "don't put anyone else down" rule in this response, hinting at a weak character.

Winner Answer I think the thing that bothers me most, and it doesn't happen often, is when a problem lingers too long. I don't think there's room in most successful organizations for unresolved problems. I like to find good solutions as quickly as possible so we can get on with the business of the organization.

Critique This response offers a real answer but not a debilitating one. It gives the interviewer a reasonable response but doesn't cause worry about applicant's ability. It reassures the interviewer that applicant is committed to quality and timeliness.

QUESTION 47

What do you do when you know you're right and others disagree with you?

Analysis This question probes an applicant's ability to work with opposing viewpoints and to tolerate the accompanying stress. It also probes applicant's comfort and ability when handling conflict.

Killer Answer First, I try to figure out a way to convince them that I'm right. If that doesn't work, and it usually does, I try to see if there's a way to work around their objections so they don't interfere with what I know to be the right approach.

Critique Aside from smacking of egomania, this response has several other problems. It implies that if applicant cannot gain compliance from those with opposing viewpoints he or she will do what is necessary to have it applicant's way. The response suggests a lack of ethical standards when faced with a difficult or conflict-laden situation.

Winner Answer First, I make sure I have enough accurate information to maintain my position. Once I'm really convinced my perspective is the one to go with, I pay close attention to the particulars of the opposition's objections. I try to reason with them by looking at the situation from their perspective. Given mutual commitment I find agreement can eventually be reached.

Critique This answer does several things. It shows that applicant approaches conflict resolution from a problem-solving, win-win perspective. It shows that applicant is open to change if that's what is called for. Finally it shows that applicant takes a collaborative approach to solving difficult problems.

QUESTION 48

Do you feel qualified to be successful in your position, and if you don't, what will you do to compensate for your deficiencies?

Analysis Like any question that asks about weaknesses, this should be handled carefully. To acknowledge that you have major shortcomings that would interfere with your work will put you out of the running. If there are minor areas to work with, those might be mentioned, although unless your silence involves misinterpretation, it's better to wait until you're on the job to shore up the necessary areas.

Killer Answer This position is a piece of cake. I could do it with my eyes closed. I think if you hire me you'll be surprised at how quickly I'll be able to deliver for you. There isn't any part of this job I can't do.

Critique Although at face value this response may sound strong, the interviewee is guilty of overkill. In addition to arousing suspicion that there may be something troubling beneath the surface, applicant also creates doubt about the potential match. If applicant is so extraordinarily capable of doing this job, perhaps the job is not enough of a challenge.

Winner Answer Although I'm sure that there are things to learn—there are in every new job—I think you'll find that I'm a quick study. I've got the skills, and I believe the talent, to meet your needs and I don't see any real obstacles in my way.

Critique While acknowledging the need to learn some new things, applicant presents confidence in his or her ability to do the job at hand.

QUESTION 49

Finish this sentence: Successful managers should. . . .

Analysis This question is designed to assess your potential for growth within the organization. Even if the job you are applying for has no managerial responsibilities, your response will give the interviewer insight into your managerial potential—and insight into what it might be like being your manager.

Killer Answer To really stay on top of things I think a successful manager needs to know more about the work than the people being managed. That's the only way to maintain control over your employees—to know more than they do. Once you lose ground it's impossible to gain it back. You have to stay one step ahead of your troops.

Critique The first problem is that applicant makes the managerial relationship sound adversarial, not cooperative. The bigger problem, however, is suggesting that it is possible, let alone advisable, to know more than every employee in your charge about everything they do. Anyone in tune with the times and rate of change in technology, information dissemination, and organizational processes knows that this approach is impractical and self-defeating.

Winner Answer A successful manager needs to be able to analyze situations quickly, determine appropriate responses, and take action. Most important, though, I think, is a person's ability to read people. Each employee is unique. Knowing that and adapting your approach to one that will work is what successful management is all about.

Critique In very few words this response details applicant's approach clearly and confidently. It suggests that applicant has a way of managing that works. Finally, the response suggests an understanding of how difficult management can be—a sentiment any manager is happy to hear.

QUESTION 50

How well do you work under pressure?

Analysis Obviously, the question is a direct approach to an applicant's response to pressure.

Killer Answer I thrive on pressure. The more chaotic things get, the better I like it. After all, these days there's no success without pressure—it's a dog-eat-dog world. I have a much bigger problem with boredom. If there's nothing to do I can get lazy; but pressure, no problem.

Critique This one falls into the "Is this person for real?" category. Aside from being unbelievable it has a negative tone and suggests that without acute pressure the applicant will be unmotivated.

Winner Answer Anyone who's doing work that's worthwhile will experience pressure on the job at times. I can handle a reasonable amount of pressure, and even extreme pressure when the circumstances demand it. The key to handling pressure for me is finding ways to manage situations to alleviate the intensity of the pressure—that way it doesn't interfere with my productivity. I know pressure comes with any job and I work well under pressure when it's necessary.

Critique This response suggests that applicant has realistic expectations about the nature and level of pressure on the job. The response is strong without being overly solicitous. Applicant presents a view of someone who has handled pressure in the past and has developed strategies for coping effectively with pressure on the job.

POWER PREP STRATEGY III

We have already said that preparation is the linchpin of power interviewing. This exercise will ensure that you are well prepared for important questions that are likely to be asked.

The first part of this activity rates your level of preparation for each question listed. The second part helps you shore up answers that are not as strong as they could be.

You will rate your preparation for each question on a scale of 1 to 5. A score of 5 means that you are fully prepared to answer the question. A score of 1 means you are quite unprepared. A score of 3 means you are moderately prepared. When scoring yourself, consider both content and delivery. For example, consider question 1: "Why do you feel you can be successful in this position?" If you know you can be successful and know how to convey your belief, give yourself a rating of 5. If you are confident about your ability to succeed but are not sure how to articulate your belief, give yourself a 3. If you're not sure about your potential for success *and* are unsure about how to convey your thoughts on it, give yourself a 1.

Each item that is rated 3 or under needs some attention if you are serious about having a power interview. If content is the problem, you need to spend some time searching your history (or your mind) to come up with a strong response. If delivery is the problem, you need to practice your responses until you feel as confident as possible about them.

When you've finished rating, transfer your scores to the coding sheet, noting which questions need content work and which delivery work. When you are finished, you will have a blueprint of what to do to strengthen your responses.

Category 1: Aggressiveness and Enthusiasm

1. Why do you feel you can be successful in this
   position?   1   2   3   4   5

2. What is your greatest strength and weakness, and
   how will these affect your performance here?   1   2   3   4   5

3. Have you ever been put on the spot by a professor
   or advisor and felt unsure of yourself? How did you
   respond?   1   2   3   4   5

4. Have you ever received a grade lower than you ex-
   pected? If so, what did you do about it?   1 2 3 4 5

5. For job advancement would you consider an
   advanced degree?   1 2 3 4 5

6. What competitive activities have you participated
   in? Were they worthwhile?   1 2 3 4 5

Category 2: Communication Skills

7. How do you go about influencing someone to accept
   your ideas?   1 2 3 4 5

8. What experience have you had in making oral presentations? How do you rate your oral presentation
   skills?   1 2 3 4 5

9. How would you compare your oral skills to your
   writing skills?   1 2 3 4 5

10. What do you least like about writing a term paper?   1 2 3 4 5

11. How should supervisors and subordinates interact?   1 2 3 4 5

12. How would you be described by a close friend?   1 2 3 4 5

13. How do you get along with coworkers?   1 2 3 4 5

Category 3: Record of Success

14. What do you consider your most significant accom-
    plishment and why?   1 2 3 4 5

15. Under what conditions have you been most success-
    ful in your undertakings?   1 2 3 4 5

16. How hard do you work to achieve your objectives?   1 2 3 4 5

17. Has competition had any positive or negative impact
    on your accomplishments? How?   1 2 3 4 5

18. What do you consider your earning potential to be
    five years from now?   1 2 3 4 5

Category 4: Rational Thought Process

19. What are the most important features you are look-
    ing for in a job and why?   1 2 3 4 5

20. How do you think our company determines success? 1 2 3 4 5

21. What is the most intellectually challenging thing
    you are looking for in a job and why?   1 2 3 4 5

22. What is the most intellectually challenging thing
    you have done?   1 2 3 4 5

23. How did you determine your career choice?   1 2 3 4 5

24. What do you consider most valuable, a high salary
    or job recognition and advancement?   1 2 3 4 5

25. Organize your ladder of success and explain this
    progression.   1 2 3 4 5

26. What qualities would be most important in deter-
    mining whom *you* would hire for this position?   1 2 3 4 5

27. What are some of the most creative things you have
    done?   1 2 3 4 5

28. Do you agree that grade-point average is an indica-
    tion of how successful you would be in this
    company?   1 2 3 4 5

29. If you could construct your own job within our orga-
    nization, what factors would you include?   1 2 3 4 5

Category 5: Maturity

30. In what ways have you been a leader?   1 2 3 4 5

31. In your adult life what accomplishment has given
    you the most satisfaction?   1 2 3 4 5

32. What determines your personal choices, and would
    you agree that others should use the same criteria? 1 2 3 4 5

33. What would you do differently if you were to start college again?   1   2   3   4   5

34. What have been your greatest disappointments and how did you respond?   1   2   3   4   5

35. What are the most important rewards you expect from a job?   1   2   3   4   5

36. Under what circumstances have your associates relied on you?   1   2   3   4   5

37. What do you feel it takes to be a professional?   1   2   3   4   5

Category 6: Planning and Organization

38. How did you prepare for this interview?   1   2   3   4   5

39. What are your personal long-term and short-term goals? How did you determine them? How did you prepare to meet them, in the long run and the short run?   1   2   3   4   5

40. What is your personal and professional five-year goal?   1   2   3   4   5

41. How would you go about creating a plan for your unit or department if you were in charge?   1   2   3   4   5

42. What is your long-term occupational goal?   1   2   3   4   5

43. How important are details to you?   1   2   3   4   5

44. How would you change your planning for the future if you could?   1   2   3   4   5

Category 7: Reaction to Pressure

45. If you were selling a product and had a customer who was complaining about poor service, what would you do?   1   2   3   4   5

46. What kinds of situations really get you down?   1   2   3   4   5

47. What do you do when you know you're right and
    others disagree with you? 1 2 3 4 5

48. Do you feel qualified to be successful in your posi-
    tion, and if you don't, what will you do to compen-
    sate for your deficiencies? 1 2 3 4 5

49. Finish this sentence: Successful managers should. . . 1 2 3 4 5

50. How well do you work under pressure? 1 2 3 4 5

Coding Sheet

Code each of your scores for the 50 items in the following spaces. For each
item on which you scored 4 or above, add a checkmark, indicating that you are
prepared to respond strongly to that question. For each item on which you
scored 3 or below, place a C next to those items for which you need more content and a D next to those for which you need to improve your delivery. Place
a CD if you need more content and improved delivery.

```
1. __   2. __   3. __   4. __   5. __   6. __   7. __   8. __   9. __ 10. __
11. __ 12. __ 13. __ 14. __ 15. __ 16. __ 17. __ 18. __ 19. __ 20. __
21. __ 22. __ 23. __ 24. __ 25. __ 26. __ 27. __ 28.    29.    30. __
31. __ 32. __ 33. __ 34. __ 35. __ 36. __ 37. __ 38. __ 39. __ 40. __
41. __ 42. __ 43. __ 44. __ 45. __ 46. __ 47. __ 48. __ 49. __ 50. __
```

Use the coding sheet as a guide to fine-tuning your interview performance.
Focus first on the items that need improvement both in content and in delivery, next on those items that need just content, and finally on those that need
just a stronger delivery. Once you improve your performance on a question—
you are the best judge—check that item off on the coding sheet. Once you've
replaced all your letter codes with check marks, you're finished! There are
many questions you can't anticipate in an interview: every interview is
unique. The questions presented in this chapter are predictable. There's a good
chance you'll get asked each of them in one form or another. But there will be
times during the interview when you'll have to think on your feet. By preparing your responses to the 50 key questions you save your creative thinking en-
ergies for the unanticipated questions. The preparation you do with the
questions in this chapter will allow you to enter the interview with confidence
and an ability to perform far above the average applicant.

4

The Key Business Trends for the 21st Century

Americans, and American businesses, love trends. Even more than trends, we are enamored of catchwords, words that conjure up images of success and prosperity. In the 1980s the word was *excellence*. Companies were committed to excellence, researchers were in search of excellence, and successful employees were purveyors of excellence.

While the concept of excellence, and its implications, still dominates the corporate landscape, it is losing ground in the career marketplace. In the early 1980s when Peters and Waterman's *In Search of Excellence* became a best-seller, clever job applicants began quoting from the annals of "the excellence books" to woo their prospective employers. Although the principles of excellence are sound and make good sense to most forward-thinking organizational leaders, the word has lost its punch. Most interviewers have been so bombarded with it that their eyes glaze over when it is uttered. In fact, we heard of one business school professor who forbids reference to any of "the excellence books" in his students' research papers because they have become so prevalent.

The astute job applicant would be wise to note the oversaturation of the term. It would be foolish and self-defeating to abandon the concept of excellence in the workplace, but it makes sense to think of more original ways to articulate its virtues.

In the 1990s the word *excellence* was replaced by the word *vision*. Not coincidentally, many consulting firms that specialize in helping organizations create and articulate their visions sprouted up in the nineties.

Having vision implies having foresight, a view of the future that determines today's actions. Vision is a picture in the mind's eye of a potential to be attained. When an organizational leader has vision, it

138

means that he or she knows where the organization is going and what it is going to take to get there. When an employee has vision, it means that he or she has at least a commitment to an organization's future, and perhaps a handle on it.

High-technology companies have been fond of the word and the concept for some time. Apple Computer Company was founded and run in the early 1980s on the vision of its cofounder Steve Jobs. Although that vision eventually ran aground, the concept and its power are still revered. When Digital Equipment Corporation built its experimental plant in Enfield, Connecticut, it named the street on which it stands Vision Drive.

When corporate leaders talk about the transformation of their companies, transformations increasingly common in this age of mergers, buyouts, and retrenching, they discuss their vision as the driving force of the company.

You may be wondering what all this has to do with your job hunt. While you obviously can't be the visionary for an organization you are not yet a part of, there are several ways the notion of vision can help you.

First, since the concept is popular, it can help you if you talk about the importance of vision for the organization and the individual. Current corporate lore suggests that if the organization does not have a vision to propel it, it is going nowhere. An individual lacking vision is headed for a comparable fate. More important, understanding and appreciating the vision of the leaders of an organization you are courting can provide great opportunity in an interview.

Showing the interviewer what you have to offer that contributes to meeting the needs of the customer will make a favorable impression. In addition, conveying an appreciation for the CEO's vision of customer service will enhance the likelihood of your being seen as a potential corporate match.

So vision is "in," and it is possible that you may be asked in an interview to articulate a vision of yourself working in the position for which you are applying. You should be prepared to respond with an answer that shows your appreciation of the value and importance of having and sustaining vision.

In this chapter you will be briefed on twelve key business trends for the 21st century. Incorporate these trends into your own vision and adapt them to what you know about the thrust of the company to which you are applying. Chances are your vision will overlap with the vision of the leaders of the organization, and more important, with the vision of your interviewers.

And while you're tracking trends and talking with interviewers, keep your ear to the street for the next big trend and begin incorporating it into your personal vision for your future. Remember, one trend sure to impact the impression you make in the job market of the 21st century is your ability to manage your own career.

TREND 1

Global Competition

Unless you've had your head in the sand you know that America's most successful companies have been facing stiff competition from all over the world, particularly the Far East. Elimination of trade barriers in Europe in the early 1990s has meant increased competition from Europe too. The competition faced by U.S. corporations means that in order to survive and thrive into the next century, companies and the people who work in them must become globally comfortable. This doesn't mean you need to speak German and Japanese (although that wouldn't hurt). What it does mean is that you need to have a global perspective and that you need to convey that perspective somehow in the interview. You need to show the interviewer that you understand and appreciate how what happens in the world has an impact on your company and what happens in your company has an impact on the world.

You should let your prospective employer know that you are willing to travel abroad if your work demands it. In fact, most observers of life in corporate America believe that the typical CEO of the future is likely to have had some experience overseas. In an increasing number of companies an overseas assignment has become a prerequisite for movement up the organization. U.S. companies will continue to export U.S. services, including banking, accounting, engineering, management consulting, data processing, advertising, and law. One of the reasons is that U.S. service industries offer advantages in scale, market reach, capital depth, and technological prowess.

The extent to which you can demonstrate your understanding that the world has become "a global village" (McLuhan) will influence your chances in the corporate marketplace. The extent to which you can demonstrate your willingness and ability to adapt and respond to life in the global village will have an impact on your desirability. The more knowledgeable you are about other countries and the ways they work, and the more comfortable you are working with them, the more desirable you will be.

So pervasive is the notion of global competition that some observers believe that, in the future, corporate lines of demarcation will replace national ones. The Singer sewing machine is an example of shifting boundaries. The shell is made in Cleveland, the motor in Brazil, the drive shaft in Italy—and it is assembled in Taiwan. Recent movements toward democratization in East Germany and Poland suggest that the homogenization of the world and the notion of corporations replacing countries is not farfetched. Although we're still probably a few decades away from corporate states instead of nation states, there is no doubt that any significant product or service produced and marketed in America will face competition from abroad. Your understanding of global complexity and your willingness to engage in global competition will set you strides above applicants who think only locally and nationally.

The economics of the global marketplace and the impact of that economics are staggering. Consider the fact that in 1960 the United States was responsibile for generating 50 percent of the world's gross national product. In 1995 the U.S. figure was 25 percent. In economic terms it truly is a new world.

Of particular significance is the growth of the Asia Pacific region. Consider China—Shanghai in particular. Twenty million people live in Shanghai and the city's infrastructure is exploding in a way that will make New York City seem like a small town. Currently 300 skyscrapers are being built. In the Pudong district alone $6 billion is being invested in building roads, ports, and telecommunications infrastructure. The Chinese government predicts it will install about 100 million telephone lines in the next ten years. Traffic patterns (a sign of economic shift) are also rising in the Asia Pacific region. In fact, 40 percent of world passenger growth in the next 15 years will be from the Asia Pacific region. There are 15 new airports under construction or development in that region. (You may be landing at one of them soon.)

The telecommunications infrastructure is exploding too. In 1997 there were 4 million mobile phone users in Korea—up from 1 million just a few years ago. By 2015 Korea will invest $60 billion dollars in telecommunications infrastructure. Indonesia will invest $10 billion by 2000. In 1998 the Asia Pacific region will be the largest market in the world for cellular services, with 70 million subscribers. By 2000 it will be 80 million.

The financial statistics are also staggering. There are 10 million credit card holders in China. The People's Bank of China forecasts 200 million card holders by 2000. The number of credit card holders in India is close to 2 million and on the rise. In Thailand there are 120 different types of credit cards.

From transportation, telecommunications, and financial services perspectives, the Far East will have the most dramatic growth, and consequently the most job opportunities for citizens of the world—including the U.S. Many American companies in these industries and others see their greatest opportunity for growth in the Far East.

TREND 2

The Flattening of Organizational Frameworks

Tell a corporate recruiter that your professional goal is to move up the organizational hierarchy and you may get laughed out of the room. In the company of the late 1990s, hierarchies are giving way to flatter organizational structures that require managers and other employees to take more responsibility with decidedly less authority. There are more people being asked to take roles that involve wearing many hats and fewer people sitting at the top of the hierarchy watching others do the work. The U.S. company of the 21st century is the hands-on company. Recruiters don't want to hear your lofty goals about someday being the head of a division. They want to hear about your willingness and ability to work as part of a team, to solve problems, and to make things happen. The more willing you are to start at the bottom and work your way up—or work your way in—the better. Corporations are inundated with new MBAs wanting to start at high-level positions. While the MBA remains a valuable credential for entry into the better companies, an attitude that it gives you special privileges is dangerous. Today's leading companies want applicants who know that career ladders are splintering and being replaced by bridges that can lead to more valued positions in the organization. Many good jobs are available to those willing to pay their dues in exchange for ownership (either actual or symbolic) in the company. The key is showing that you understand how things are and that you are willing to participate.

The hierarchy is being replaced by the network. Consequently, organizations are looking for people who can manage relationships up, down, and across departmental and division lines. High-potential employees will be those who are comfortable as network managers rather than those concerned only with pleasing those above them. A profile of corporate giant U.S. West illustrates this point. An article in *U.S. West Today* described the ideal candidate as someone who is neither a specialist nor a generalist, but "a totalist." A totalist is a sort of Renaissance employee who knows a lot about one area, and a bit about many others, and is comfortable moving freely from one thing to another. An ability to manage relationships across division lines and throughout the shrinking hierarchy is considered a vital skill, as is an ability to perform a wide variety of tasks.

Demonstrating an understanding of the shift from hierarchies to flatter organizational structures will convey to your interviewer that you have an up-to-date understanding of contemporary organizational life and its demands.

Many organizations are spending a lot of money on what's called reengineering. Reengineering has become a popular approach for transforming organizations and often results in the flattening of an organization's hierarchy. The principle behind reengineering is simple, although many companies are not finding it easy to employ. The idea is that by focusing on the core processes required to produce a product or service, the organization can be more effective and efficient. This streamlining of activity often eliminates the need for the role of the traditional manager who oversees the work of others; elimination of such jobs means lessening the number of layers in the organization's hierarchy. One of the greatest challenges for many organizations tackling reengineering is the elimination of what are often referred to as stovepipes. Stovepipes are arbitrary boundaries between one function and another that serve to protect the turf of individuals. The belief is that by removing the boundaries or stovepipes and focusing on the key tasks needed to reach a goal, the organization will be more competitive. There is more to reengineering and flattening of organizational frameworks than is detailed here, but the important thing from your perspective is to be sensitive to this trend and the propensity for many organizations to operate lean and not be prone to hiring people who merely oversee the work of others.

TREND 3

Managing Diversity

Demographic indicators suggest that the core of the U.S. workforce is changing dramatically. The days when white males were a company's entire roster of employees are over. Increasingly organizations will be staffed and run by women and people of color. (The term "people of color" refers to all people who do not fit the category "white" and is used to ensure that people of all cultural backgrounds are included in the discussion.) Whether you are a white male, a woman, or a person of color, the extent to which you are comfortable working with people from diverse backgrounds will dramatically affect your chances and your success. Gaining familiarity and feeling comfortable working with people from different cultural and gender backgrounds will help you negotiate your way into higher positions and succeed there.

Managing diversity involves more than expressing a belief in women's rights or in equal opportunity for all. It involves a commitment to understanding the ways in which people different from yourself operate. It involves an understanding of the ways people from other cultures communicate and negotiate in the world around them. The classic example cited in classes on cultural diversity (classes well worth taking) is the Hispanic child who is repeatedly reprimanded by the white teacher as being disrespectful for not looking the teacher in the eye while being scolded. What the white teacher does not know is that looking down when being spoken to by an adult is a sign of respect in that child's world. Consequently, the teacher's ignorance of cultural difference perpetuates the problem.

There are many subtle and less subtle cultural differences at work in an increasingly diverse workforce. The first step in improving your ability to manage diversity is to become aware of your own behavior and its cultural bias. One vivid example of cultural bias at work comes from research conducted by three sociologists, Carol Word, Mark Zanna, and Joel Cooper, reported in a 1974 issue of the *Journal of Experimental Social Psychology*. In the experiment white job interviewers interviewed black and white applicants. Through observation in a one-way mirror, researchers observed that the white interviewers treated the blacks differently from the whites by sitting farther away, making less eye contact, sitting in a less direct position, and ending the interview significantly sooner. When debriefed on the interview, most of the subjects were unaware of the subtle differences with which they treated the two groups of interviewees. Recent high-profile discrimination suits alleging unfair employment practices related to race in some major corporations suggest that the observations made in 1974 regarding discrimination in the workplace are just as relevant today as they were then. Most experts agree that the first step in improving your ability to manage diversity is to gain a better understanding of your own bias, both conscious and subconscious, and overcome aspects of your behavior that could lead to unfair treatment.

Understanding how people from various backgrounds operate can enhance your ability to perform on the job. As in the Hispanic example just given, a lack of this understanding can lead to many ways of misunderstanding and inappropriate responses in the workplace. For example, one cultural group gaining prominence in the past ten years in the U.S. is the Japanese. Anyone who thinks that understanding the Japanese is not important to U.S. business would seem, to any savvy businessperson, to be quite out of touch. At last count the Japanese owned four of the five biggest banks in the world and a good portion of the commercial real estate in almost every major U.S. city, including New York. If you are in any major business, from cars to computers, you are likely to run into a chief competitor who is Japanese. You also may find yourself working for the Japanese, as did everyone at Columbia Records when Sony Corporation bought it. In their 1974 book *Foundations of Intercultural Communication,* Sitaram and Cogdell reported on some differences between Asian and white American styles of communicating. Some ways in which people with Asian backgrounds might communicate differently than white Americans are using tradition to support an argument, focusing on group welfare versus the individual, valuing silence in conversation, and avoiding direct criticism. This last point is a good example of the way disconnects can occur between someone from a white Anglo-Saxon background and someone raised in an Asian culture. In the Anglo-Saxon culture giving direct criticism in a work situation is considered effective feedback, if it is delivered with constructive intent. However, the Japanese don't operate that way. In fact, a colleague of ours tells a story about being an American in a Japanese company and being told by his boss to "take another look" at the report he submitted. In the world of the Japanese manager these words were intended to mean, "I'm not happy with the job you did on this report—you need to redo it." Our American friend, oblivious to the cultural norm in the Japanese company of delivering criticism indirectly, misread the situation and made no changes in a report that his boss had found unacceptable.

Even more important to managing diversity than understanding foreign competition is understanding the groups likely to provide large segments of the U.S. workforce in the future. The Department of Labor recently reported that the number of black Americans in the workforce increased from 8 million in 1965 to 12.4 million in 1985; the number of Hispanic workers nearly doubled between 1975 and 1985, to 7.7 million from 4.2 million. These growth trends have continued between 1985 and 1995 and the U.S. Department of Labor's Bureau of Labor Statistics predicts that these trends will continue in this fashion through the year 2005. In fact, by 2000 nonwhites will account for one-third of all new workers. Some estimates suggest that only 15 percent of the new entrants to the workforce will be white males. Thus blacks, Hispanics, and Asians will make up a significant proportion of the U.S. workforce. If you are a member of one of these groups, the challenge is to establish your value in what can often prove to be a hostile environment. If you are white, the challenge is to heighten your awareness and find ways to communicate and coexist with an increasingly diverse workforce. You need to persuade prospective employers that you can help their company thrive in the inevitable diversity of the next century. If you doubt the importance of sensitivity to diversity in the American workplace, consider the impact of that insensitivity on Texaco in the late 1990s. The revelation that senior level executives were using insensitive, racially biased language caused a great uproar. The further revelation that this insensitive language was only the tip of the iceberg in what came to be a corporate culture rife with racial discrimination has cost the company in many ways.

TREND 4

Understanding and Using Computers

As computers and computer networks become more sophisticated, people working in the companies for whom those systems are designed need to become highly proficient in their use. If you're uncomfortable with computers or unfamiliar with their use, you'd better get over it or start looking elsewhere for work (perhaps in some other century). The computer revolution is as much a part of contemporary life in corporate America as the copy machine or the telephone. Many jobs once performed by people, or currently performed by people, will be taken care of in the future by a network of computers. Your job will be to manage the use of the computers effectively, and to find better ways to use them, regardless of your work. The more you can demonstrate an understanding and mastery of computer technology, the more likely you will be seen as a potentially valuable player.

Just as it is difficult to find a middle class American home that does not have a VCR, it will be difficult to find an executive team in the 21st century that does not rely on computers. Computer technology is moving so fast that those not committed to keeping up will be left in the dust. For example, a new advancement in computer application is decision technology. In one of its applications, collections of computers and databases, called executive information systems, provide instant in-depth information on every aspect of a company for strategic planning and corporate decision making. While some CEOs are shying away from this technology because they fear it will stifle their creativity, many are embracing it, acknowledging the power it has to make their decisions more prudent. Three new tools have emerged through the use of the microcomputer to help managers think more clearly about their businesses. First, *cognitive mapping* is used when decision makers are unclear about what decisions need to be made. It is essentially a brainstorming tool to help clarify what needs to be done. Second, *decision mapping* helps decision makers consider the impact of a decision on a wide range of organizational variables. And third, *microworld technology* constructs a simulated model of an organization to help users consider a broad range of organizational moves. Although each of these concepts existed before the widespread use of the microcomputer, they are enjoying increased popularity as they become simplified and more usable. In terms of the job search, the computer revolution offers many opportunities. Getting your résumé registered with one of the many networks that have surfaced to make the job-matching process easier for applicants and those filling positions is a wise move for anyone seeking to get his or her name out in the marketplace. Becoming adept at surfing the Internet is a skill worth mastering both for the purposes of getting information about prospective employers and positioning yourself as someone who knows how to use computer technology to full advantage.

A friend of mine is a computer enthusiast who has mastered the use of the Internet for obtaining information about anything. He happens to be from Norway. Having mastered the net, my friend gained access to and began reading the local newspaper of his hometown newspaper in Norway before it was even available at the local newsstand. One day he read of a car accident that occured near his parents' home. He phoned home from New York City to inform his parents that their neighbor had been in a car accident, but was not badly hurt. While this may not seem like earth-shattering news, it serves to emphasize the extent to which a savvy computer user can use technology to gain information—and competitive advantage.

I recently used this story to convey to a client of mine, an executive in a commercial transportation company, how he could use technology to competitive advantage. The executive, a 30-year veteran in his company, was (like many of his counterparts at the top of the corporate ladder) not very computer-literate. Like many of his high-level colleagues he grew up in corporate environments where the most technically sophisticated tools were the typewriter and the slide rule. He was technologically averse and believed he had nothing to gain from becoming computer-literate—even though the president of the company was always on him to develop his computer skills to become more proficient with e-mail. His decision to hone his computer skills surfaced after I told him the story of my Norwegian friend. This executive was responsible for a spinoff of his company that was based in Russia. The thought of his being able to access information about what was going on in the region before his direct reports in Russia was enough to get him focused. He was cruising the net in no time.

It is easy to see that without a basic knowledge and appreciation of computer technology and a willingness to stay abreast of new developments, you can be left behind. While the executive in my story was able to delay his computer literacy because of his stature in his company, he eventually saw the wisdom of bringing his skills up to speed. Don't imagine that as an entry level or mid-level job applicant you have the same prerogative. You don't.

The serious contender in a power interview would be wise to develop an up-to-date knowledge of computer applications and their potential impact on any target organization.

TREND FIVE

Teams, Teams, Teams

Anywhere you go in corporate America today you hear talk of teams. All the buzz about participatory management has made way for the teamwork revolution. By all indicators, the manager of the past who orders underlings around will be replaced by the orchestrator, the leader who effectively creates, monitors, and assists groups of people working together to get the job done. Your success as a member of a team will be determined by your ability to work cooperatively with other team members toward a given end. Your success as a potential organizational leader will be determined by your capacity to empower others, instill a sense of commitment, and help articulate a team vision that reflects the broader organizational vision. Your ability to couch your skills in terms that suggest you have what it takes to work successfully in and manage teams will greatly enhance your chances of getting the highly sought-after jobs.

Teamwork in the workplace was initially an American idea. However, ironically, it was not implemented here and was not taken seriously until recently. After World War II, however, the Japanese, determined to rebuild their economy—and comfortable with the notion of teamwork because of their cultural emphasis on the group rather than on the individual—embraced the idea wholeheartedly. In fact, some analysts suggest that the Japanese comfort with teamwork is the foundation of their current prominence in the world market.

U.S. corporations have made recent attempts to emulate their Japanese counterparts with the introduction of quality circles (groups that attempt to solve organizational problems by holding brainstorming sessions); employee involvement programs; and with a decidedly American twist on the concept, employee stock ownership plans. A prime example of such efforts is a joint project of General Motors and Toyota in Fremont, California, where Japanese-style team management has been extraordinarily successful.

Productive and profitable as it may seem, teamwork in the U.S. workplace is struggling. Americans, it seems, are decidedly individualistic and have trouble, by many accounts, in making teamwork work. In fact, many companies report unfavorable results from their efforts to switch to a team approach. In spite of its failings, however, team management is considered to be, by many accounts, the wave of the future in the United States. In 1987 the U.S. General Accounting Office found that 70 percent of 476 large companies were using the simplest form of teamwork, quality circles. Boeing, Caterpillar, Ford, General Electric, General Motors, and Digital Equipment Corporation are only a few of the major companies that strongly espouse the teamwork concept. Teamwork strategies and talk of cooperation have been resisted by middle managers, fearful of losing their roles, and by union leaders, fearful of losing their power. However, recent threats to their security by foreign competitors who use teams freely have gradually changed the attitudes of many opponents of participation. A recent convention of the United Auto Workers, in which workers voted by a large majority for employee involvement, signals that worker participation and teamwork are here to stay. In the 1990s one would be hard-pressed to find a major corporation that has not dedicated significant human and financial resources to the development of teamwork among its managerial and employee ranks.

Although you don't need to be an expert in the technology of employee involvement, you do need to have an understanding of the basics and be prepared to present yourself as a team player with strong team management skills. Many organizational leaders are looking for people who are comfortable with the team concept and have some understanding of how it works. The more you know about teamwork and the various forms it can take, the more attractive you will be to an increasing number of organizations committed to the teamwork concept.

Here's a quick tutorial on one of the more prevalent models for teamwork: the high performing team. These teams have several characteristics. First, they have a clear purpose or mission, often articulated in a mission statement that reflects the broader mission of the organization in which the team resides and gives the team its sense of direction. The team has clearly articulated goals for the overall team and roles for individual members are made clear and explicit. Second, high-performing teams have dynamic leadership: leaders who know how to harness the individual energy of team members so that problems get solved in a higher-quality way than any individual member would be capable of. Third, communication in a high-performing team is open and honest. Differences are aired and dealt with collaboratively. Decisions are made with the input of all team members and when possible consensus is used to move the team forward on important decisions. Last, the team climate is one where people enjoy being part of the team. Successes are celebrated and failures are used as an opportunity to learn and do better next time.

Demonstrating an understanding of the characteristics of high-performing teams can serve you well in an interview, as can demonstrating an understanding of what it takes to create and sustain such a team.

TREND 6

The Service Obsession

If U.S. corporations pay attention to demographic trends, and they do, they know that what will separate the winning companies of the next century from the losing ones is service. In many segments of the population, consumers are screaming for service. Dual-career couples with young children want quality service. The huge mass of people entering their "golden years" demand service. Ken Dychtwald, CEO of Agewave and an expert on the needs and interests of aging America, spends much of his time consulting with companies on how to modify products to meet the needs of older consumers. For example, one of his suggestions to the Avis car rental company was to provide a special service to customers over a certain age, such as a car at the airport door with their luggage already in the trunk. It's service like that, suggests Dychtwald, that the public wants—and will pay for. Demographers tell us that it is these two segments of the population, the baby boomers and the aged, that make up the lion's share of the buying public; and they're the ones with the most money to spend. If you want a job with a leading company, you'd better know this, and you'd better let your prospective employer know that you are committed to quality service because you recognize it as a key to organizational prosperity.

Service comes in many forms. Most of us can readily think of times when we've had inferior service. It's much harder to think of an incident of especially good service. Marketing experts tell us that one of the key variables determining customer loyalty is the experience the customer has during the transaction. Even industries whose primary competitive edge is the service they supply seemingly wear blinders when it comes time to make service-minded decisions. The shift in the 1980s to automated tellers in banks is a good example. While customers find them handy during off-hours, research suggests that given the option, a customer would prefer to interact with another person— not a machine. In many banks, the shift to automated tellers at the teller cages has resulted in loss of customers.

When I was shopping for stereo equipment recently, I was more careful than usual. I had recently been burned by an inexpensive tape deck that warbled almost from the day I bought it. When I brought it in for repair I was told, as I was handed the bill, that there was nothing wrong with it; it just needed a cleaning. I brought it home only to find the warble unchanged. This time I went to a shop that was new in the area but was developing a reputation for high-quality service. During my conversation with the salesperson I was told that the shop had made a commitment to outstanding service—and that to date it had not charged any customer for a single repair and hoped to continue the policy as long as possible. The salesperson got my attention and my business.

Service is intangible and therefore sometimes elusive. Yet it is clear that the United States has suffered a crisis in service in recent years and that a key to a company's prosperity will be to make people feel good about how they purchased something as well as what they purchased.

As we move to more of a service economy it becomes evident that without attention to service no company will survive and thrive. Whether you're approaching a hardware store for the best way to winterize your house or a clever salesperson to help you pick out your next interview outfit, chances are you will buy at—and come back to—the place that gave you the best and most informed service.

For example, one of the industries to blossom in the midst of America's service-obsessed consumerism is the overnight mail business. The successful companies in this business base their success on providing timely, efficient, and effective service. Federal Express, one of the giants in the field, knows that its success is no accident. It has an extensive service-training program for all new employees. Anyone in the company who has contact with customers receives two to five weeks of customer service training, with follow-up training later on.

Since service will be the life blood of any organization in the near and distant future, it makes sense for you to develop a keen appreciation for it. You would also be wise, when interviewing with any organization, to think about ways in which high-quality service manifests itself in that organization and to let your interviewer know of your sensitivity to it.

TREND 7

From Brawn to Brains

It's always been true that the best companies rely on a pool of highly intelligent and resourceful people to run their organizations, and the intelligence factor has become increasingly important. There was a time when working harder could deliver, but that is no longer true. Companies are looking for people who work smarter. It is the belief of many in corporate America that intellectual rather than physical capital will be the driving force behind successful companies. People who can manage information well will be the stars. Demonstrating an understanding of organizational systems in all their forms; of telecommunications; and (as mentioned earlier) of computers, both hardware and software, will set the smart applicant apart from the crowd.

An understanding of and adeptness at creating software will be extremely valuable. Knowing how to encode knowledge, to convey information through software, will be a skill highly valued in the techno-workplace of the 21st century.

But software is merely a vehicle for an information society. What is perhaps most striking about the changes in the business world is the magnitude of the change. Consider this observation from an Associated Press article of July 23, 1989, by Peter Coy: "In 1866 international communication was only for the elite. It cost one hundred dollars to send a twenty-word cable from New York to London on the first undersea cable. Today it costs one dollar to send about four thousand words over the same route using an ordinary personal computer and modem." The information float has collapsed, and the flood of knowledge in and out of organizations is more intense than ever. Even more significant than mastery of software is ability to navigate your way through cyberspace. The proliferation of the Internet and the creation of intranets—self-contained mini-Internets within organizations—will be so prevalent in the 21st century that people who can't plug in and navigate their way need not apply for work. This is particularly important for those of you in the middle years of your career who were not weaned on computers. As alluded to earlier, you need to become computer-literate and, more important, computer-comfortable so that you continue to upgrade your skills as the systems around you become more sophisticated. Those of you in your mid-career years should be aware of the competition you face. For example, my twelve-year-old son uses a computer as though he was born with a mouse in his hand. He moves freely in and out of chat rooms talking with people all over the world about any topic of interest. In a few years he and his friends will be competing with you for jobs and if you don't want to be left in the dust you had better start competing with him on how to use cyberspace to access and use information.

The key to global competitiveness is knowledge. Gaining and using information more quickly and more effectively will be vital to a company's prosperity. Job applicants who demonstrate an understanding of the importance of knowledge and the ability to gather, process, and use information will be worth a great deal.

Because of the information explosion, education and training have become a side industry of many companies. IBM spends $900 million a year on education and training. In this field, many companies have operating budgets larger than those of many colleges. Why is there such a commitment to education and training? Companies realize that without brainpower they will lose out. For example, most managers of engineering believe that, without constant upgrading, a typical engineer's knowledge base will be obsolete within three years.

Showing an appreciation for the nature of the knowledge explosion and a commitment and ability to remain up to date in your personal knowledge base will take you far in the information age and in the power interview.

TREND 8

Quality Is Job One

This by now familiar quotation, "Quality is job one," from one of America's leading automakers reflects a growing concern in the corporate world. Management guru Tom Peters caught the attention of the U.S. automobile industry when he decried the inferiority of his GM truck, talking about "minor" problems like a failed four-wheel drive light and a rattling glove compartment lock. Peters's popularity and his widespread appeal sent a message to the industry that he—and the American consumer—would not tolerate poor quality. The mythology around quality seems directly related to the prosperity of a company. For example, there's a story about a Honda employee who, on his way home from the factory, would stop and adjust the windshield wiper blades on any Hondas he passed to ensure that they were "just right." The contrast between Peters's story about his GM truck and the Japanese employee's attention to detail paints a disturbing impression of the two competitors' attention to quality.

Increasingly, U.S. companies are concerned about producing high-quality products. Quality control is a major concern of most companies, and corporate leaders are looking for people who know how to create conditions that foster an organization-wide commitment to high quality. So adamant about quality and its impact is management seer Peters that his book *Thriving on Chaos* gives the following example (p. 72): "A brochure is going out to customers. You've already missed your deadline. Five thousand have been printed, inserted into envelopes, addressed and sealed, and are packed and ready to be taken to the post office. Your small unit's cash flow is pinkish to red in hue. And then you discover a single typo on page two, in the small print. Should you walk past it or act? Easy. Act—throw it out!"

You might think this tactic is a bit overzealous, but it illustrates how adamant people are becoming about quality. This is not just Peters's view: he reports it is held by many of the most successful companies in America, large and small. Even if you think Peters takes the emphasis on quality too far, the important thing to note is that being a zealot for quality can only help your chances in any forward-thinking company. In fact, one of the key concerns for many organizational leaders is finding ways to build in commitment to quality and develop strategies for motivating employees toward producing consistently high-quality products. If you want to gain points with your interviewers, show them you have ideas about ways to ensure quality in your work and to foster quality in the work of those around you.

Quality assurance, the buzzword for programs and departments that work on improving quality, has established itself so firmly in corporate America that it has become a potential career path for some workers. Peters reports on one welder who became so involved in quality control that he was asked to make a presentation on quality at a company-sponsored Japanese Management Association meeting; eventually he became a supervisor and an articulate spokesperson for quality throughout the company.

One thing is certain about the companies that survive into the 21st century: Quality will make the difference. Most competitive companies are keenly aware that a major reason the Far East has so successfully infiltrated the U.S. marketplace is that products produced in the Far East have often been of better quality than comparable U.S. products. An applicant's understanding of and commitment to quality will assure the interviewer that applicant has an appreciation of the competitive marketplace that will help keep the company on top.

TREND 9

The Human Side

Companies are showing unprecedented concern for employees, becoming more sensitive about child care, parental care, employee assistance, and health care. Employees will find their organizations increasingly responsive to their needs. Lest the reader or job applicant think that a wave of altruism is spreading through the land, consider the wise words of *Megatrends* author John Naisbitt. Naisbitt says that social change occurs in America only when economic necessity dictates. If organizations are treating people better, one explanation is that they must do so in order to survive. Several factors suggest the truth of this. First, there is an impending labor shortage. Most demographic indicators suggest that in the early part of the 21st century there will be a shortage of qualified people to fill crucial jobs in many organizations. This means that if they've got good employees, they had better keep them. The second factor also has to do with demographic factors, with a different slant. Because of the flattening hierarchies and emphasis on teams discussed earlier, organizations will need fewer middle managers. With fewer opportunities for advancement, organizations must find other ways to keep employees. One strategy, used by an increasing number of organizations, is a developmental model that looks at employee growth as a means of retention. By getting to know employees better as people, management can find out what their needs and interests are and how it can provide incentives other than promotions to keep them happy.

The successful organizations will be the ones that can hang on to valuable people. By showing your prospective employer that you have an understanding of human motivation and how to keep other employees happy, you present yourself as someone who can help solve the looming problem of employee shortages.

One interesting development since the 1980s has been the embracing of the human potential movement by business. The human potential movement, developed in the early 1960s by psychologists, philosophers, and other practitioners, concerns itself with stretching the boundaries of human consciousness by experimenting with alternative ways of being. In the 1970s the movement continued to develop momentum, but it wasn't until the 1980s that it became part of mainstream America. In the nineties, acceptance of the principles of human potential has become part of the fabric of many organizations as they grow increasingly concerned with finding ways to increase and improve employee performance. In fact, it was in the early part of this decade that many organizations recognized the importance of tapping into the individual motivation and needs of employees as a way to harness the potential of the organization.

Most notable in this shift toward "honoring the individual" is the work of management guru Stephen Covey, whose writing and widely used programs on personal effectiveness have paved the way for self-improvement as a legitimate workplace activity. Some observers attribute the acceptance of human potential principles to demographic factors, suggesting that the children of the 1960s will be the corporate leaders of the 21st century and that they're bringing their values with them. Others argue that it is older, wiser leaders who are bringing human potential into the workplace. Whatever the causes, it is clear that wherever you look in business today, leaders are articulating the need to take care of people. All the best-selling management books— books written by and about the leadership of corporate America—give attention to people a first priority. In his book *Leadership Is an* Art, Herman Miller Furniture Chairman Max Depree talked about the role of an organizational leader as one who enables and empowers people. Leaders, he maintained, need to create environments that foster the development of high-quality relationships between individuals, among work group members, and between employees and clients and customers. Depree's beliefs about what it takes to be successful in corporate America are being echoed in every forward-thinking company, large or small.

As an interviewee you can be sure that whatever position you're seeking, those on the other side of the fence will be looking for someone who is sensitive to the needs of people. Present yourself as someone who appreciates the relationship between good people skills and the bottom line and you will make great headway in your search.

TREND 10

Value-Added

Downsizing has had and will continue to have a major impact on the workforce of the future. With the fat trimmed it becomes essential that the lean organization be one where every player makes a significant contribution. The increasingly popular term *value-added* reflects this mentality. Value-added means that everyone in the company will be able to demonstrate in specific terms the impact of his or her contribution to the strength and prosperity of the organization. The growing belief that a key to any company's success is the ability of the leaders and the employees to utilize one another to the maximum so that each player makes a clear measurable contribution is the core of the value-added mentality. The value-added concept is an outgrowth of the accountability movement of the 1970s and early 1980s and has been spurred on by economic hardships. The result is a reshuffling of what gets done in many organizations and by whom. The value-added movement has restructured many industries and spawned some new ones. For example, during the 1960s and 1970s many companies developed large human resource departments where they employed internal consultants to help with management development, training, and other human resource functions. With the value-added movement came questions about the contribution of these functions to the bottom line or the added value of the organization. Since these functions could not be tied directly to the bottom line they were considered "soft" and were often eliminated or scaled back.

I recently experienced two examples of how this concern about appearing "soft" and not adding value has impacted the way people view their work. The first had to do with a man whose role had developed into a support role for various projects (not an unusual scenario in organizations that are flattening themselves and trying to eliminate redundant roles). The man, while busy performing tasks for many groups, felt he was performing valuable services for many people; yet he felt vulnerable. The primary reason was that he was keenly aware of the value-added mentality prevalent in his organization. He was, from his own perspective, not as visibly value-added as he needed to be because he was not clearly accountable for project results but rather helping others achieve results. In his annual performance review he expressed this concern to his boss. His boss agreed that he needed to be more results-oriented and more accountable for hitting the bottom line. As such his role shifted to focusing on a few critical projects and not the broad-based support of his previous year. Unfortunately those who depended on him in the past lost a valuable asset. However, the employee feels more secure in his role and believes his value-added is abundantly clear.

The other situation that drove home the prevalence of the value-added mentality was a meeting I attended with a human resource group within a company which felt under attack for not being value-added. This department, like many human resource departments, had failed to change with the times and saw themselves primarily as administrators and monitors of human resource programs. The problem with this HR definition is that information technology has made the need for many of the administrative functions obsolete. The HR group, now aware of increasing obsolescence, is going to great lengths to reengineer the department, eliminating many administrative tasks and focusing on building skills as agents of change—a much needed role in the contemporary organization. Success in making this shift will ultimately determine whether the group remains intact or is eliminated as a nonvalue-added frill of the organization.

To replace these internal roles, consulting firms have appeared whose purpose is to provide human resource functions to companies that need them. In the human resource company, the human resource function is a value-added function since it is the product or service that the company provides. What has occurred is the elimination of certain roles and the emergence of companies whose primary role is the external performance of eliminated internal functions.

When approaching organizations you need to be keenly aware of the value-added mentality which predominates in so many of them. You need to present a case for joining the organization that highlights what your value-added contribution would be. In fact, recent advice on the part of many recruiters to people seeking to work in organizations where there is no specific opening is to gain entry into the organization through the sales department. If you want to get your foot in the door, they say, start out in sales, where the value-added connection is most obvious. Remember, in an increasingly competitive world, the bottom line, more than ever, is the bottom line.

TREND 11

Keep It Clean—Ethics in the Workplace

A few years ago a cartoon was widely circulated on many university campuses in which a student was trying to sign up for a course on business ethics. The caption read: "Make up your mind: Which is it, business or ethics?" The cartoon is no longer relevant. Today, a business student would be hard pressed to find a program in which business ethics was not at least an elective and most likely a requirement.

These days there is much talk of ethics in corporate hallways. Recent scandals on Wall Street and the failure of some large corporations to meet their moral obligations have left an impression of deteriorating conditions. Increased intolerance by the public of environmental abuse and financial misconduct has sent a message that many company leaders are heeding. Those perpetuating or willing to tolerate unethical behavior in their organizations are seeing the impact that consumer boycotts and bad press can have. The applicant aware of the new ethical standards spreading through the corporate sector would be wise to communicate an appreciation of those standards during the selection process.

More than a minimal level of ethics will be required in the organization of the 21st century. Because of such organizational changes as shrinking numbers of employees, management-labor alliances, employee involvement, global joint ventures, and quality improvement programs, organizations will need unprecedented levels of trust and integrity in the workforce. Fierce competition is not likely to disappear, but organizational leaders will also be concerned with creating alliances within and between companies that result in win-win situations. This changing mentality will create a job market in which high moral and ethical standards in applicants will be highly prized.

The interesting thing about ethics is that you can't see it, taste it, feel it, or hear it, yet we have our own sense of it. Like fingerprints, your ethics are unique—and you leave them everywhere you go. No one compromises or changes your ethics but you. Ethics cannot be prescribed, nor can they be feigned. Developing a strong sense of ethics will protect you in the marketplace. No job, promotion, or amount of money is worth a compromise of your ethics. Solid companies know this and will respect a person with high ethical standards. In fact, putting ethics first often strikes a chord that resonates far and wide. Consider the case of Aaron Feuerstein, President and CEO of Malden Mills, a textile mill in eastern Massachusetts. When the company experienced a serious fire that nearly destroyed it, many people feared their livelihood was gone. Instead of closing the mill, this CEO used the disaster to revitalize the company and exercise the highest ethics. In fact Feuerstein refused to stop paying employees—even when there was no work to be done. Hailed as a hero in the national press, he claimed that he was merely doing the right thing. Besides continuing to run his company, which has successfully risen from the ashes, he now lectures on "The Bottom Line vs. The Right Thing" and explains how his philosophy of treating employees as his most valued asset is propelling Malden Mills to renewed productivity and growth.

Developing and living by a high level of ethical standards makes good sense for you as a person and as a professional. Communicating a high level of moral and ethical standards in an interview will help you find the best jobs in the best places—where ethics count.

TREND 12

Risky Business

The shift toward greater accountability should not be confused with the notion of playing it safe. With the onset of global competition, the information explosion, and the emphasis on creativity and innovation, U.S. companies are looking for people who are not afraid to take risks. The ability and the willingness to take shrewd yet calculated risks is an important attribute for anyone seeking power positions in the contemporary organization.

In a recent speech to MBA candidates at the University of Pennsylvania's Wharton School, Raymond W. Smith of Bell Atlantic Corporation said: "Don't make the mistake of confusing what a big company will tolerate with what it rewards. . . . Taking the safe road, doing your job, and not making waves may not get you fired (right away at least), but it sure won't do much for your career or your company over the long haul. We're not dumb. We know that administrators are easy to find and cheap to keep. Leaders—risk takers—are in very short supply. And ones with vision are pure gold."

The key to remaining competitive in the global market, by most accounts, is developing and fostering know-how and inventiveness—trying new things. Companies concerned with holding their own and increasing their market share want people who are visionaries—people not afraid to find a new angle on an old problem.

While applicants who convey an ability to manage a unit effectively may get some of the jobs, those with the best chances will be the ones who convey an ability to lead others into an ambiguous and volatile future.

In the battle for market niches in the coming decades, innovation and risk taking will determine the winners and losers. One vivid example of the potential for great loss or gain is the electronics industry. American manufacturers lost an enormous market niche in VCRs by not fine-tuning their machines as quickly as the Japanese did. Consequently, not a single VCR is manufactured in the United States today. High-definition television (HDTV) is in a similar position to that of the VCR ten years ago. Most observers in the industry believe that the key to conquering this potentially enormous market will be the extent to which U.S. companies can harness their creativity, move forward with innovative designs, and take the risks required to launch such a massive endeavor.

Risk taking in the contemporary company is fueled by accepting and embracing creativity in the workplace. Until recently creativity was regarded as something a limited number of people possessed. People considered creative would most often be found in research and development or in marketing. As companies seek new ways to compete and thrive in the marketplace, organizational leaders are looking for people who can find creative solutions to a broad range of organizational problems. From shortening production processes to naming products to eliminating the need for stockrooms (it's called on-time production), companies are relying on creative ways to cut costs and improve productivity. Not only have creativity and the risk taking it has spawned become acceptable in the contemporary workplace, but they are coveted.

An applicant's ability to convey a sense of adventure, a knack for creative thinking, and a willingness to take risks will not go unnoticed in the forward-thinking company of the early 21st century. However, you need to be careful not to portray yourself as reckless. It's not the gamblers who will win the best jobs but rather the smart risk takers. I was recently talking with the CEO of a mid-size company in the transportation industry who spoke of the need to promote more risk taking in his organization. In the next breath he articulated the need for people to "make their numbers." When I probed him about this seeming contradiction we had an enlightening conversation about the need to balance risk taking with pragmatism. In fact, he said that that was what he was really looking for, people who understood the need and could demonstrate the capacity to strike the right balance between accountability and risk. Convey an understanding for and an ability to manage this delicate balance and you will get the attention of the right people looking to fill the key positions in their organizations.

POWER PREP STRATEGY IV

This chapter presented a primer on the key trends for the 1990s. You can be sure, given the volatility of the world economy and the struggle for U.S. companies to redefine themselves, that these trends are on the minds of corporate leaders everywhere. Interviewers will be looking for applicants who understand the trends and appreciate their significance. Power Prep Strategy IV will help you identify which trends that you are familiar and comfortable with and which ones need further attention. For the answers to some of the questions you may have to refer back to the text; for others, you may have to do some research on the company; and for some, you'll have to search your own background. Complete the following questionnaire on the 12 trends and you'll be ready to use them to your advantage in the power interview.

Trend 1: Global Competition

What does the term *global competition* mean to you? _____

_____

_____

What experience do you have in dealing with people from other countries?

_____

_____

_____

What involvement does the company you are interviewing with have with companies and markets of different countries? _____

_____

_____

What impact might increased global competition have on the work of the company you are approaching? _____

_____

_____

Trend 2: The Flattening of Organizational Frameworks

How does the flattening of organizational frameworks change a person's access to career ladders in an organization? _____

_____

_____

What does the organizational chart of the company you're approaching look like? _____

_____

_____

Where does the position you are applying for fit on the company's current organizational chart? _____

_____

_____

Trend 3: Managing Diversity

What is your ethnic background, and how does that affect the way you view the world? _____

_____

_____

How does your being male or female affect the way you view the world and the workplace? _____

_____

_____

What stereotyped attitudes do you hold about people different from yourself, and what can you do to rid yourself of them? _____

_____

_____

What experiences have you had in working with people different from yourself, and how have you managed these relationships? _____

_____

_____

Trend 4: Understanding and Using Computers

What kinds of computer hardware and software do you know how to use?

_____

_____

_____

How have you used computers in the past to make a work project more efficient or effective? _____

_____

_____

Trend 5: Teams, Teams, Teams

Does the organization you're interviewing with have any formal team development programs (for example, quality circles or employee involvement)?

_____

_____

_____

Have you been involved in work teams in the past or in any sort of organized
team activities (for example, sports or fundraising)? If so, how successful
were you? _____

_____

_____

What skills do you have that would make you a valuable contributor to an organization's teamwork (for example, group dynamics or interpersonal communication)? _____

_____

_____

Trend 6: The Service Obsession

List ways in which you have provided extraordinarily good service to a customer or client. _____

_____

_____

Does the company you're interviewing for have an articulated view on service (for example, in its organizational goals, mission statement, or slogan)? If so, what does that tell you about the company's approach to service? _____

_____

_____

What do you have to say about your appreciation of the importance of service, and how can you articulate it in an interview? _____

_____

_____

Trend 7: From Brawn to Brains

What experience have you had in managing large amounts of information?

_____

_____

_____

In what ways does the organization you're approaching depend on having up-to-date information? How does it go about getting it? _____

_____

_____

What information-gathering and organizing technologies are you familiar with (for example, networks or software programs) and how could you use them in your prospective organization? _____

_____

_____

Trend 8: Quality Is Job One

Does the company you're approaching have an articulated position on the importance of quality (for example, in its mission statement or slogan)? If so, what is its position? _____

_____

_____

What experience do you have with quality assurance or quality control? Do you have any stories you can tell about contributing significantly to the quality of the development or delivery of a product or service? What are they?

_____

_____

_____

Trend 9: The Human Side

What do you know about what motivates people at work (other than money, which is a given), and what examples do you have that show you to be a good

motivator of others? _____

_____

_____

Do you have any experience creating work incentives in an organization? If you don't, what are your ideas about it? If you do, what are some examples?

_____

_____

_____

What experiences do you have in your background that show you have strong

human relations skills? _____

_____

_____

Trend 10: Value-Added

What products and/or services does the company you're approaching consider

to be its primary source of income? _____

_____

_____

What organizational functions are considered critical to the delivery of the company's products and/or services? _____

_____

_____

What skills do you have to offer that make a direct contribution to this organization's production and delivery of services? _____

_____

_____

Trend 11: Keep It Clean—Ethics in the Workplace

What is your personal code of ethics for the workplace? _____

_____

_____

Does the company you're approaching deal with any sensitive areas that might increase the need for a clearly articulated stance on ethics? _____

_____

_____

Does the company you're approaching include a statement on ethics in its mission statement or in any other formal literature? If so, what is its position?

_____

_____

_____

Trend 12: Risky Business

What experiences do you have that show you are capable of creative risk taking? _____

_____

_____

How does the company you're approaching view creativity and risk taking? Is there any evidence that these traits are valued in employees? _____

_____

_____

Remember, these are significant trends in almost every employer's mind. Bring them up whenever you get the chance and you will be seen as someone in tune with and capable of handling the challenges of the future.

5

Winning the Interviewer: How to Read, Impress, and Win Over the Decision Makers

THE CLINCHER CONNECTION

Interviewers make great effort to be as objective as possible, but they are only human. When asked how they decide between two equally qualified candidates for a position, most corporate interviewers confess the truth. They pick the one with whom they feel the stronger connection. This somewhat fuzzy notion, "the connection," is worth your attention. As an interviewee you are faced with a difficult chore. Your job, in addition to answering questions in the strongest way possible, is to influence the person across from you to make a decision in your favor. Observers of human behavior and interpersonal relationships have spent many years trying to explain why each of us is more attracted to some people than to others. Explanations range from the scientific (genetics) to the ethereal (karma). Chances are good that neither of these extremes will help you. What is helpful, however, is to consider a variety of factors that might well sway the interviewer in your favor.

Knowing Your Target

Knowing your target is easy, but most people don't take the time to do it when preparing for an interview. What is required is willingness and ability to search out information about your prospective target and to use it in a way that sets you apart from the crowd.

For example, say you set as your target corporate giant AT&T. You may think you are approaching an old, established institution steeped in bureaucracy. You may, if you are not careful, approach this organization as it existed before divestiture, as the regulated monopoly it once was, and make assumptions about its corporate culture based on that image. Or you may approach it as the single entity it was before 1996. You'd be dead wrong.

If you had done your homework, you might have read the cover story in the June 19, 1989, issue of *Fortune* Magazine, featuring Bob Allen, the CEO of AT&T. In that article you would find that the operating procedure for AT&T was to adapt and adjust to change, not to stay as is. You'd find that there has been a dramatic shift in the way the organization is run, away from the centralization of Allen's predecessor to a decentralized team approach. You'd learn that Donaldson, Lufkin, and Jenrette, a key consulting firm for AT&T, stated, "A lot of good young bulls below top management will carry the company into the 21st century." You'd also know, if you were up to date, that the company broke up into three companies in 1996, with three distinct cultures. With that information, you'd have a much better chance of having a winning interview.

Understanding Organizational Cultures

Understanding the culture of the organization you are approaching can be a key to getting your foot in the door. Finding creative ways to reach the people with the power can set you apart from the crowd. For example, we heard of one man determined to get a job in a top advertising agency but unable to gain access to its decision makers. After several traditional approaches he tried something different. He took an old shoe of his, shined it up, and sent it to the prospective employer with a note that read, "Just wanted to get my foot in the door." Now we wouldn't recommend this tactic to you for any other industry, but in this case it was the perfect entrance into an organization whose top concern is hiring people with imagination.

When you choose to work for a winning company you will probably encounter an organization deeply entrenched in its culture. A company does not become one of the elite overnight. More than likely there are a range of organizational customs and rituals that define the company. Understanding what makes an organization tick before observing and responding to its customs in the course of the interview process can make a big difference.

You can learn about an organization by keeping your eyes open on your way to the interview. The physical surroundings, the building, the landscaping, the layout of the offices, and their content can tell you a lot about the culture of the organization. Looking carefully at these things will tell you what working in the organization might be like and can help you build your case for a match.

For example, we knew of one woman who was traveling around the country doing research on female presidents of small companies. She was on her way to see a woman who had started a very creative company and was surprised when she arrived at the entrance of a typical industrial park. She expected a more aesthetically pleasing environment, given the nature of this woman's company. Her expectations were confirmed when, cruising through the mass of prefab aluminum warehouses, she spotted a white stucco building off in the woods adjacent to the park. She didn't have to check the address. She knew she had found her target.

The inside of a building, particularly the way workstations are set up, will tell you about the culture of the organization too. For example, walk into any traditional U.S. industrial factory and you'll see people lined up in rows of bolted-down tables performing their routine tasks. The supervisor will be walking up and down the aisles. The clock will be on the front wall, and bells will ring to signal breaks, lunch, and the ending of shifts. And they wonder why employees act like schoolchildren! The way work is doled out and set up will tell you about what working in an organization will be like and can help you navigate an interview.

Transfer the preceding scene to a corporate setting and you'll see what we mean. We know of one Fortune 500 insurance company where employees fight over inches of office space. Status is so tied to the amount and location of one's workspace that no one will give an inch. One woman spent two months without a desk because the one to match her newly appointed position was not in stock; she refused to work at a smaller one, and the company refused to give her an oversized one for the interim period. In this organization, with a bit of keen observation, you could tell how valued the job you were applying for was by the location and dimensions of your workspace.

Like the creative company started by the entrepreneur, the schoolhouse factory, and the territorial insurance office, the companies you approach will have settings that represent their culture and the values of their leaders. Pay close attention to these symbols and you will be on your way to determining the cultural pulse of the organization—and to making the connection you need to get the offers you want.

Making Contact

Research on human behavior in the past 50 years suggests how differ- ent people view the world in different ways. You may think this has nothing to do with the interview process, but understanding and re- sponding to these differences can help you. Each of us is surrounded by a perceptual screen, a filter if you will, that processes what we see, hear, and feel a split-second before we experience it. Being able to identify the perceptual screen of the interviewer quickly can go a long way in helping you make the critical connection.

One way to understand differences is through NLP (neurolinguistic programming). NLP is a simple way to read a person's style that can enhance your ability to connect with the person. Therapists have long used NLP as a way of making clients feel more at ease. It has recently enjoyed success as a way for salespeople to make the all-important link with the customer. The link you make with an interviewer can help add to the impression that you may be a good person for the organiza- tion. Understanding and using NLP can help create that link.

Consider that by behaving in a certain way you can convince some- one you are a certain type of person. Great actors have long appreciated this simple truth. Anyone who has seen Dustin Hoffman in the movie *Rainman* can attest to Hoffman's mastery, his ability to persuade us that he is an autistic savant. It wasn't until I saw a rerun of *Sixty Minutes* that I realized what Hoffman had done. The TV segment profiled three sa- vants, people with limited everyday skills who had achieved extraordi- nary mastery in a particular area, to the point of being called geniuses. One of the savants, like Hoffman's character in *Rainman,* had remark- able mathematical ability. He looked, sounded, and acted just like Hoff- man's characterization of the savant. What Hoffman did, to persuade us we were watching a true savant, was to match his behavior, his sound, his actions, and his affect, to the point that we believed what we saw, heard, and felt while watching the movie.

Some psychologists would call it behavior modeling. This is an ap- proach to training developed by industrial psychologist Albert Bandura whereby a trainee masters a skill by closely observing and replicating the actions of a master. The payoff is that the trainee appears to be like the person being modeled. If one of the ways to make a connection is to make the interviewer feel that the two of you are alike, behavior modeling can help do it. This may seem artificial to some of you, but it is a way to overcome the artificial barriers created by interviews. If it feels comfortable to you, use it; if not, don't—it wouldn't work anyway.

NLP can also create a sense of connectedness with an interviewer. Although mastering NLP can take some time, the basic principles are simple. You can master NLP with some practice and find it helpful in all sorts of relationships beyond, as well as during, the interview. The key aspect of NLP is identifying a person's primary sensory orientation. There are three basic orientations: visual, auditory, and kinesthetic. Visuals rely heavily on their eyes: they like to see what they are thinking about. Auditories rely on their ears more, want to hear things clearly, and are more dependent on words for gaining understanding. Kinesthetics are hands-on and depend on getting a feel for something before passing judgment.

Here's an example of how to identify someone's NLP orientation. I run a workshop series in a beautiful old Victorian house. When new participants begin a series, I invariably get comments and questions about the setting. I can often tell from these comments and questions what a person's NLP style is. When someone says, "Look at this place; isn't it something?" I know I'm with a visual person. When someone asks, "What do you know about the history of this place?" I know I'm with an auditory person. When someone says, "Imagine what it was like living in this place years ago," I know I'm with a kinesthetic.

Imagine you are being interviewed for a job you want. The questioning is going well, and you want to be sure to leave the interviewer with the feeling that you would be a good match for the position. One way is to identify the interviewer's primary orientation (visual, auditory, or kinesthetic) and act the way that your interviewer understands best. This may seem an unfair strategy, but it doesn't have to be. We're not suggesting that you be someone you're not. That would probably backfire on you. What we're suggesting is that in an artificial situation and limited time (talk about unfair!) you use all resources available to you to make things go your way.

If you're comfortable using this information, here's how to proceed. Pay attention to the language your interviewer uses when asking questions to determine whether you are sitting across from someone who is primarily visual, auditory, or kinesthetic.

Visuals experience the world most dramatically through their eyes; consequently they think and speak with visual cues. When presenting ideas, visuals are most likely to talk about how things appear to be. When zeroing in on an idea they would tend to talk about getting a focus on something. Visuals will present a scenario for you to respond to by giving you a picture of a situation. When asking about your ideal job they might ask what the perfect job situation would look like. When presenting difficult problems for you to solve they would ask you to see yourself in the situation. A visual interviewer might ask about your perspective on a given organizational problem or ask you to outline an approach to solving the problem.

Auditories experience the world most vividly through their ears; consequently they think and speak with auditory cues. When presenting ideas they may ask you to listen carefully in order to understand a situation. When zeroing in on an idea they would tend to talk about tuning in to what's going on. Auditories will present a scenario for you to respond to by asking you what a situation sounds like to you. When asking about your ideal job they might ask to "hear" what you want out of a job. When presenting difficult problems for you to solve they would ask you to discuss possible solutions. An auditory interviewer might ask you to elaborate on your opinion on a given organizational problem or to articulate an approach to solving that problem.

Kinesthetics are very tactile; they experience the world by touching and feeling what's going on around them. Consequently, they think and speak with kinesthetic cues. When presenting ideas they might ask you to get a feel for a situation. When zeroing in on an idea they would tend to talk about really getting in touch with what's going on. Kinesthetics will present a scenario for you to respond to by asking what you sense is happening. When asking about your ideal job they might ask where you think you might fit in the organization. When presenting difficult problems for you to solve they would ask what your grasp of the situation is. A kinesthetic interviewer might ask you to see if you can get a handle on an organizational problem or get hold of an approach to solving it.

As you read these three examples, you probably found one of the three to be more natural. Your response to each is a clue to what your orientation is. The one that feels most comfortable is probably the one that matches your personal style. That's important to keep in mind because it's part of who you are and how you communicate. More important, though, is being able to read others' orientations so you can respond to them in a way that leaves the impression that you understood them or even identified with them.

People with a visual, auditory, or kinesthetic orientation will present a broad range of ideas and scenarios without deviating from their primary orientation. One way to begin to use NLP effectively for interviewing is to create a list of words you might use if you are operating in a given mode. The preceding examples used seven typical words or phrases for each orientation. Think of some others and keep them in mind the next time you're talking with someone. You'll be amazed at how easily you can identify whether someone is visual, auditory, or kinesthetic.

Another way to understand differences and make a connection by overcoming them is to pay attention to the extent to which people are action-oriented (versus observant) and feeling-oriented (versus cognitive). Many years ago psychologist Carl Jung postulated that these two continua—active versus observant and feeling versus thinking—were the basis for understanding key differences in human nature. Since then many theorists have developed models about learning and human behavior based on the Jungian concept.

Imagine once again that you are sitting across from an interviewer and the questioning is going well. You want to make that all-important link with the person opposite you. Two things will help you make a stronger connection: Is the interviewer feeling- or thinking-oriented, and is the interviewer action-oriented or observant? Those who are feeling-oriented will show an interest in the "people side" of a situation. They will focus on the elements of a problem that involve the impact on the human factor. Their concern, regardless of the problem, will tend to be on how its outcome will affect the players involved. They are not necessarily more humanitarian than others, but they bring a perspective to situations that highlights the impact on people and their responses.

Those who are thinking-oriented tend to focus more on the task at hand than on the people involved. They tend to think analytically about potential outcomes of a situation in terms of the product or project in question. Their concern, regardless of the problem, is on what the concrete results will be. They are not necessarily less concerned about people, but they tend to look at situations from a bottom-line perspective.

In addition to the feeling-thinking continuum that differentiates some interviewers from others, there is also the action-observant continuum.

Those who are action-oriented like to focus on immediate results. They tend to forgo the long range for the short term. They are more likely to be concerned with the impact of a decision on the present than on its far-reaching ramifications. They are more concerned with the here and now than with the future. While they can appreciate the importance of long-range planning, it is not their top priority.

Those who are observant tend to think analytically and systematically. They are concerned with the whole picture and the long term. They know that results matter, but they believe that the means by which those results are attained will, in the long run, also make a difference. Like chess players, people who are observant tend to think in terms of steps and are focused on the impact of each step on subsequent moves.

Now you may be thinking that any successful businessperson will, out of necessity, be all of the preceding, depending on the situation. You are right, but most people tend to be more on one end of each continuum than on the other. Paying attention to whom you're talking to, and paying attention to the end of the continuum they seem to be working from, is important. It can help you to understand them, effectively respond to them, and ultimately, win them over.

Personality and the Power Interview

A significant trend in recent years is increasing emphasis on finding the right personality fit for jobs. A popular tool for assessing personality for the best fit, both formally and informally, is the Myers-Briggs Type Inventory, a personality test designed to identify preferences that define your personality. Unlike many personality tests, the Myers-Briggs is not intended to identify abnormalities or distortions in personality, but simply differences. It is based on the personality theory of Swiss psychologist Carl Jung, who theorized that there were differences in personality among the normal population. In the 1940s Katherine Briggs and her daughter Isabel Briggs Myers built on Jung's work to create the Myers-Briggs Inventory, which is now a standard in many organizations. It is considered by many organizational psychologists to be one of the most valid identifiers of psychological difference, and it is viewed by many corporation managers as a legitimate way to diffentiate people in terms of work style and occupational and organizational fit. The MBTI is so commonly used that it is not unusual to hear people in corporate hallways talking about being an S or an N or a J or a P. If you overhear this kind of alphabetical shorthand and you don't know what people are talking about, chances are you've inadvertently eavesdropped on a Myers-Briggs conversation!

The reason so many have embraced the principles of the MBTI—and the reason it's important for you to understand it on at least a rudimentary level—is that it is an easy way to understand the potential fit for a given task or job.

Here's a quick tutorial on the four continua of the Myers-Briggs and the 16 personality types it describes.

The first continuum is extrovert (E) to introvert (I). It refers to how a person is energized. Extroverts tend to be interactive; they get involved with others, like having people around, communicate openly, and tend to view things from an external perspective. Introverts tend to prefer privacy, think things through before talking about them, and view things more from an internal perspective.

The second is Sensing (S) to Intuition (N). It refers to what you pay attention to. Sensors tend to depend primarily on the five senses, and like to focus on what is real and factual as they move through the day. Intuitors tend to rely on their sixth sense, and use hunches and their intuition.

The third is Thinking (T) to Feeling (F). It refers to what a person draws on primarily for decision making. Thinkers rely on the head, using logical systems and objective criteria to make decisions. Feelers depend on the heart, tending to use values and subjective data to make decisions.

The fourth is Judging (J) to Perceiving (P). It refers to one's orientation to the external world. Judgers are planful people who like to regulate and control the activities of their lives. Perceivers tend to be spontaneous, prone to adjust and adapt their activities as they unfold.

This review gives the reader a rudimentary understanding of the four continua, but this is only the tip of the iceberg. Know that there are people who dedicate their lives to better understanding the complexity implied in this simple description of personality differences.

Since the MBTI has been so widely embraced, we will take it further and review the 16 personality types from two of the many vantage points possible. First let's look at how preference influences one's work style.

Extroverts tend to like variety and tend to shy away from routine. They prefer work environments that include other people and they act quickly.

Introverts prefer to work on one thing at a time and enjoy having quiet time to think things through. They tend to act in a mindful way rather than jump to action.

Sensors like practical tasks and focus on the details of work. They come to conclusions step by step. They seldom make errors about facts.

Intuitors thrive on innovation. They like exploring new territory and thrive on change. They are not afraid to make mistakes and like to learn from experience.

Thinkers rely on principles for determining action and choices and make decisions impersonally, focusing most on what they believe is the right thing to do.

Feelers rely on values to determine actions and choices and make decisions with the impact on people foremost, focusing on what they believe is the fair and compassionate thing to do.

Judgers work planfully and often drive toward closure and completion of tasks. They use structure and systems to get work done.

Perceivers, in contrast, work adaptively, keeping things open until the perceiver is confident things have evolved sufficiently. They use flexibility and adaptation to get work done.

Now we will describe the 16 types and how they prefer to work.

- ISTJs prefer work that is controlled and requires attention to detail. They function best in environments that emphasize accountability, productivity, and fact-based problem solving.

- ISFJs prefer work that requires deep commitment and a sense of service. They tend to do well in positions that require a lot of behind-the-scenes work.
- INFJs prefer work that involves the betterment of other individuals, groups, or communities. Their focus is on being a caring, helpful presence in the world.
- INTJs are visionaries. They are idea people who function best in environments that focus on the possibilities.
- ISTPs prefer work that requires speed and do so most often in a fiercely autonomous fashion. They do best in work situations that require a self-starter.
- ISFPs prefer work that involves helping and supporting others in their environment. They are low-key and do best in environments that support and promote harmony.
- INFPs prefer work that serves their personal values. They function best in work situations that rely on the use of reflection, imagination, and contemplation.
- INTPs are abstract thinkers who gravitate toward work that requires frequent conceptualization of ideas. They work best in creative, challenging, thought-provoking environments.
- ESTPs prefer work that is entrepreneurial and involves risk. They function best in work that requires a multitude of decisions where the outcomes are ambiguous.
- ESFPs prefer work that puts them in the social fray. They function best in roles that require them to be outgoing, engaging, gregarious, and high-energy.
- ENFPs are people-focused. They are best in jobs that require them to use their creativity and intuition to solve people problems.
- ENTPs are high-energy, creative, challenging people. They work best in situations that require making connections between seemingly disparate things.
- ESTJs tend to be practical, multifaceted problem solvers. They work best in situations that require them to organize people and develop methodologies and systems.
- ESFJs are good mediators. They work well in situations that require them to reconcile differences between others, and because

of their capacity to mediate are often looked to to help others manage conflict.

- ENFJs are strong persuaders. They do well in roles that require influence and persuasion and do well in environments that require them to motivate others to action.
- ENTJs are leaders. They function best in roles that give them a substantial amount and scope of responsibility, and thrive in situations that demand they take charge.

The above tutorial is but a glimpse of this complex, elaborate, and increasingly popular study of human personality. If I've piqued your interest, there are many books and seminars that will better inform you on the intricacies of the Myers-Briggs. At a minimum you should know that you fall into one of the 16 categories, and your interviewer does too. You should consider the implications of the widespread use of this theory in hiring and selection processes. There's a good chance your interviewer has a certain personality type in mind for any given position. Knowing what this mindset is and responding in a way that assures you can perform—whether or not you're a type match—can make the difference between an offer and rejection.

The Importance of Worldview

Interviews are person-to-person encounters. No matter how objective the process is made to seem, ultimately people are judging people. It is reasonable to assume that the judgments the interviewer makes about the interviewee are key to the outcome. Ideally, the key judgments relate to the key aspects of the job. Unfortunately, the key judgments sometimes relate more to personal characteristics than to professional ones.

You are who you are, and there's no point in projecting an image that differs dramatically from your authentic self. However, if the subjective side of interviewing is, as we suspect, essentially Russian roulette, it makes sense for your own survival to pay attention to who the other players are. One way to understand your interviewer, and perhaps to make the critical link we've talked about in this chapter, is to pay attention to and respond to the interviewer's worldview. A worldview is a set of beliefs and attitudes a person has about a range of universal concerns. Discovering an interviewer's worldview can be particularly helpful if you find yourself sitting across from someone with whom you have little in common.

The concept of worldview is a way of organizing information about your perspective on a range of issues, a way to sort out who is sitting across from you. One's worldview includes knowledge, beliefs, and attitudes about politics, religion, sports, family, education, money, and a host of other topics. Paying attention to your interviewer's positions in these areas can help you make the personal link that makes the critical difference.

It is amazing how calling on some aspect of worldview can turn a difficult situation into a harmonious one. For example, I was recently at a luncheon with a colleague. The two of us were working on a major contract with a client who to date had been rather reticent about our relationship. On the way to the meeting my colleague and I were discussing our client's coolness and planning a strategy that might turn things around. Since there seemed to be no problems about the work we were doing, we decided to get through the business of the meeting as soon as possible and keep our ears open for any opportunities to connect through our worldviews. During dessert I asked the client if he had any children. His face lit up as he began talking about his daughter and her swim team. My colleague, an avid, award-winning swimmer in high school, chimed in with all her knowledge about swimming, coaching, and the current state competitions. We spent the next half hour talking about our families, and we left the meeting feeling more comfortable than we had felt before with this client. Our subsequent project proved successful. The work was done in an enthusiastic, cooperative mode. We attribute some of that success to the connection we made through our worldviews.

While you may not always get an opportunity to compare worldviews with an interviewer, paying attention to who he or she is and looking for opportunities to connect can make all the difference. Following are some of the key worldview categories to keep in mind.

Politics Politics is one of the stickier worldview categories. More than divulging whether you are a Democrat or Republican is at stake here. If you're not careful, you may present a bias that is perceived as contrary to the needs of the organization. A good rule of thumb is to avoid making statements that commit you to any political position. Listening can shed light on the interviewer's leanings and priorities. One man we know who was head of his previous organization's union drive highlighted his union work in his résumés and interviews. He had a difficult time finding work. Just when he was about to change his approach he was interviewed by someone who had been a union organizer in his early years. That was the last interview he needed.

The Arts During a recent vacation I asked an 18-year-old on my block to watch my house while I was gone. I was new to the neighborhood and had just met the young man. He seemed very competent and responsible, yet a bit uncomfortable with me. I knew his family and figured he was concerned about doing a good job. When I returned I asked him to come by so I could pay him and tell him what a good job he had done. He still seemed a bit nervous. I noticed he was wearing a Bob Dylan T-shirt from a recent concert tour, and I mentioned that when I was growing up I was a big Dylan fan and had a collection of his albums. The young man got excited, we talked about music for a while, and he left feeling more of a connection with me than he had when he walked in.

Many people have enthusiasms or passions for certain artists or arts activities. Often they love meeting people who share their enthusiasm; they feel an immediate kinship. Opera buffs love to meet other opera buffs; Grateful Dead enthusiasts (Deadheads) love to meet other Deadheads; stamp collectors love to meet other stamp collectors. More than similarity is involved. People feel they learn something about someone when they uncover their enthusiasms. These interests are not always visible or available to you, but they may become evident if you pay attention to comments, objects in the office, and so on.

Sports Like it or not, chances are if you're sitting across from someone who has been successful in the corporate world, that person knows a reasonable amount about sports. You may believe (rightfully) that this has nothing to do with your potential performance, yet ignorance about sports can hurt you. Often talk about sports, like the weather, is used to break the ice or to fill gaps in time. Unless you have a basic understanding of major U.S. sports—baseball, football, basketball, and yes, golf—you may find yourself embarrassingly without comment when the interviewer is trying to make you feel at ease. Lack of knowledge about sports is not the kiss of death, but it is worth your while to know the basics. (We heard of one interviewee who mistook talk of a Giant touchdown for conversation about the space shuttle.)

In America sports serve as a metaphor for business. Creative people in business will often use sports analogies to gain insight into an organizational problem or scenario. If you don't understand the basics of sports you may find yourself wondering what everyone is talking about.

Family The sanctity and value of the family used to be unquestioned. This can still be a worldview category that makes a connection (as illustrated in the story earlier in this chapter), but not always. It used to be safe for an applicant to expound effusively on the importance of family in an applicant's career. Many things have changed that view, however, including the proliferation of dual-career families and the concern that applicant may be stretched by too many family demands. While families are gaining ground in their efforts toward corporate-supported child care, other trends are emerging that give families less clout.

Many companies are concerned about the extent to which a person is family-focused versus career-focused. Recent developments such as the mommy track, the notion that women with families should be on different career tracks than those without, demonstrate this concern. While it's okay to care about your family, most employers want to believe that the company and the job come first. And it is possible that the interviewer doesn't have a family to care for and may not share or understand your commitment.

Paying attention to the interviewer's cues about attitudes toward family can tell you whether this worldview category makes for a potential connection.

Money In the free enterprise system, applicants are most likely going to meet people who place making money high on their list of priorities. Beyond this basic concern for turning a profit, however, you will find a range of attitudes about money and the discussion of financial matters. It is safe to say that the closer the business is to finance-related endeavors, the more talk of money will be evident. In industries such as banking, investments, and insurance you are likely to hear people talk at length about money because essentially it is their product. The farther you get from the money industries the harder it is to tell the difference between greed and ambition. Some people are open books about their finances and don't hesitate to talk about their activities, say, in the stock market; others consider finance questions to be a violation of their privacy. Paying attention to expressed attitudes about money will tell you which aspects of it the interviewer is comfortable with and which are off limits. You may not find the occasion to talk about money in an interview, but there are times when a common perspective will surface, creating the opportunity to form another link with the interviewer.

OVERCOMING DIFFERENCES IN AN INTERVIEW

In addition to your worldview, other factors having to do with who you are can work for or against you. You have no control over these characteristics, but you have some control over how they are perceived.

The old adage "Great minds think alike" may or may not be true, but quite often "like minds think alike." The more similar you and your interviewer are in age, race, socioeconomic and educational background, and gender, the more easily you'll be able to make a critical connection. Being different from your interviewer in any (or all) of these categories is not a reason for despair. However, it is a reason for attention. When you pay attention to the differences between you and the interviewer, your chances of getting through to the interviewer—in spite of your differences—increase dramatically.

Age

I had a woman in my office today who was worried about getting work. "Who would want to hire a 47-year-old woman," she lamented. I recently heard the same fear expressed by a graying 48-year-old man. The problem, I told them both, is not their age but the attitude about their age that they bring to an interview. I've seen men and women lose job opportunities, not because of their age, but because of the way they present their age. Statements such as "I would bring a tremendous amount of experience to this position" work much better than "I know I'm older than the typical candidate but..."

If you're sitting across from an interviewer considerably older than you, you probably need to convince him or her that you have the maturity to do the job. If you're sitting across from someone considerably younger than you, you need to convey that you are not after his or her job and that you have no problem reporting to someone younger. If you and the interviewer are a similar age, you may find a sense of camaraderie that you can tap for making a connection. But be careful! Some interviewers resent assumptions based on age. Also, be sure to let the interviewer know that you can handle reporting to a peer.

Socioeconomic Background and Status

There is no explicit class system in this country, but people find ways to identify with and differentiate themselves from certain groups. Some people take pride in coming from a working-class background, whereas others pride themselves on their privileged lineage. Also, people find ways to express their socioeconomic status by their clothing, jewelry, cars, and even the way they wear their hair. People often make assumptions about others, whether true or false, after noting artifacts of socioeconomic background. Focusing on the socioeconomic artifacts of the person interviewing you will often give you information on who he or she is or at least would like to be.

If you find yourself sitting across from someone whose background seems similar to yours, you may find ways in the course of an interview to let that be known. If you sense that the two of you are vastly different, avoid highlighting the differences. Remember, in general people are more comfortable with people they perceive to be like them than those they perceive to be different.

Race

Racial similarities and differences are probably the most difficult personal characteristics to deal with. In a culture dominated by whites there is pressure, regardless of your race, to behave in a way typical of the dominant group. If the interviewer and the interviewee are white, you probably won't think about race during the interview. Awareness of racial differences becomes evident when interviewer and interviewee are from different racial backgrounds. Remember, if the interviewer is from a racial background different from yours, he or she may have ways of communicating that are unfamiliar to you.

People often find, when they take a close look at racial differences, that different groups have different norms concerning eye contact, personal distance, body language, and other subtle aspects of communication.

The important thing when trying to overcome racial differences with interviewers is to follow their lead in the course of communication. This does not mean mimicking them, which will certainly backfire. It means letting them establish some norms about the way the two of you communicate. Doing this will demonstrate your ability to communicate with someone different from yourself, will make the interviewer more comfortable, and will avoid potentially embarrassing and damaging mistakes.

Educational Background

As with socioeconomic background, some people carry an academic identity reflecting a status level. If you attended a prestigious school, you may have access to some organizations more easily than do others. Those of you who have attended a prestigious school will find that your access does not diminish over time. I once worked with a client who graduated from Harvard in 1959. He was looking for work in a new field and was having trouble finding it. He was startled when I encouraged him to tap his university alumni association for contacts—after all, it had been 30 years. He did call his association, and to his surprise it was very responsive and helpful.

Those of you who don't have a prestigious school in your background need to be aware of bias when approaching an organization that has a history of hiring people from certain schools. Do not make the mistake of thinking that you are out of the running—exceptions are made every day. As with the age issue, the extent to which you rise above this potential shortcoming will determine your success. If you find yourself competing with Ivy Leaguers and you are not one, be sure to emphasize the quality of the education you received and how you managed to get it.

Gender

Men have long been the dominant sex (at least overtly) in the workplace. Over the past 30 years women have made considerable headway. It is now entirely possible (although statistically unlikely) that you could be interviewed for a high-level position by a woman.

If you are a man and find yourself across from a woman interviewer, you need to be aware that one of her concerns is whether you are comfortable reporting to a woman. The corporate workplace is still dominated by men, and many women have been burned by men who use gender as a weapon against them.

If you are a woman being interviewed by a man, your task is to convince him that you are as aggressive and hard-driving as the male competition.

If you are a woman and your interviewer is a woman, chances are she has had to face many hurdles to get where she is. Don't assume that being a woman will help you. Most reports suggest that women who have succeeded are at least as hard as men on other women on the way up. Chances are you will have to prove to her that you can contribute to the company.

If the interviewer and interviewee are male, you probably won't even think about gender in the course of the interview—unless you are applying for a job as a secretary.

GIVING YOURSELF AWAY

It is essential to remember that in an interview you are selling yourself. A key element of effective salesmanship is knowing and responding to the customer and his or her needs, interests, and values. You may not know it, but car dealers do this all the time. In most places, when you walk into an automobile showroom you will be sized up by your age, sex, the way you dress, the car you drove in with, and how you operate from the time you get out of your car until you enter the showroom.

Based on this analysis you will be confronted with a salesperson whom the dealership's demographers (they may not call themselves this) decide will be most likely to pitch you successfully. Imagine that you are the dealer and the car buyer is your interviewer. Although this may seem to be a reversal, it mirrors the interview situation in many ways. Although the car buyer must persuade the salesperson that the buying potential is there, the onus is on the salesperson, like the applicant, to convince the other that the product is worth the price.

YOU ARE WHAT YOU SAY

You, the applicant, are trying to present yourself as someone who fits the desires of the organization. Once again we can look at sales strategies to gain insight into how this is done. Imagine for a moment that the interviewer is a consumer of stereo equipment and you, the applicant, are a stereo merchant. It doesn't take a very trained eye to see that different stereo stores, through the image they project, appeal to different consumers.

A glance through the Yellow Pages reveals three names: The Wiz, Sound Playground, and Scientific Stereo. A brief analysis of each name brings up some fairly safe assumptions. If I am most interested in price I go to the Wiz (whose motto is, "Nobody beats the Wiz!"). If I am interested in equipment with lots of bells and whistles I go to Sound Playground. If I am interested in high-quality sound without the frills I go to Scientific Stereo. Each name, in two words, says a great deal about the image of the store and creates significant assumptions about the potential match between the seller's and the buyer's needs. You need to have a clear understanding of who your interviewer is and what his or her needs and desires are in order to persuade the interviewer that you are right for the company.

POWER PREP STRATEGY V

Organizational Cultures

This chapter discussed the importance of understanding the organization you're approaching by understanding its organizational culture. Cultural information can be found by reading the organization's literature, visiting the organization before an interview, conducting preliminary interviews, and talking with people who work there. Uncover the following information about the organization you are approaching and you will have a good grasp of its culture and of what working there would be like.

Who is the CEO of the organization you are approaching and what is the CEO like? (You can gather this information from news clips, informal conversation, networking, and so on.) _____

_____

_____

What does the way the building looks tell you about the organization's culture? _____

_____

_____

What does the way the employees dress tell you? _____

_____

_____

What does the setup of the offices tell you? _____

_____

_____

What do the internal modes of communication (for example, employee newsletters and bulletin boards) tell you? _____

_____

_____

What does the organization's image tell you? _____

_____

_____

What does the allocation of resources (who gets what) tell you? _____

_____

_____

What does the reward system tell you about who is valued? _____

_____

_____

Understanding the Interviewer's Style

In the discussion on neurolinguistic programming you were told that some people are visual, some auditory, and some kinesthetic. What ways do you use to identify the NLP styles?

Visual _____

_____

Auditory _____

_____

Kinesthetic _____

_____

What is your personal NLP style? _____

_____

_____

In Carl Jung's model of types of people you were told that some people are more feeling-oriented and some more thinking-oriented. You were also told that some people are more action-oriented and some more observant. What ways do you use to tell what a person's orientation is?

Feeling-oriented _____

_____

Thinking-oriented _____

_____

Action-oriented _____

_____

Observant _____

_____

Which of the four types in Jung's model most reflects your personal style?

Feeling/action-oriented   Thinking/action-oriented

Feeling/observant   Thinking/observant

What are the implications of your style on your performance in an interview?

_____

_____

MBTI Mini Self-Assessment

In the MBTI there are four continua. Place yourself with an X on each of the four continua, based on your perception of yourself. (Avoid dead center on each scale.)

Extrovert _____⊥_____Introvert
                                 midpoint

Sensor _____⊥_____Intuitor
                               midpoint

Feeler _____⊥_____Thinker
                              midpoint

Perceiver _____⊥_____Judger
                                midpoint

What combination of these four continua best describes you? _____

_____

_____

What are the implications for you in terms of how you will project yourself in

an interview? _____

_____

_____

Worldview

What is your personal worldview on politics, and to what extent is it likely to

match or clash with the politics of your interviewer? _____

_____

_____

Who are your favorite arts figures, what are your favorite arts activities, and to what extent are these likely to be accepted and respected where you're being interviewed? _____

_____

_____

What do you know about the major U.S. sports, what is your attitude about sports, and what if any metaphors do you use comparing the nature of sports to the nature of business? _____

_____

_____

To what extent are you able to balance work and family, and how can you show that your family's needs will not interfere with your work requirements?

_____

_____

_____

To what extent are you comfortable discussing money matters? How might your knowledge of and comfort in discussing personal finances hinder or help your connecting in an interview? _____

_____

_____

Overcoming Differences

To what extent do you consider your age to be an asset or liability in an interview? In what ways can you use your age to connect in an interview? _____

_____

_____

What significance does your socioeconomic background have for your position as an applicant? How can you use it to your advantage? _____

_____

_____

What significance does your racial background have for who you are?

_____

_____

_____

What do you know about racial differences that can help you connect in an interview with someone of a different race? _____

_____

_____

In what ways does your educational background strengthen or weaken your position as an applicant? How can you compensate for the weakness or capitalize on the strength? _____

_____

_____

How does your being a man or a woman affect your sense of who you are? How does that affect your performance in an interview? _____

_____

_____

How might your gender influence your chances in an interview? What can you do to neutralize any assessment based on gender? _____

_____

_____

6

Choosing a Work Style: Finding the Right Places to Interview

We assume that those who are interested in power interviewing are also interested in using their personal power to get the best jobs. What is the best job depends on your needs and desires. In a country such as ours that is rich in opportunity, there are many places to find the sort of success you can gain by harnessing your personal resources. In this book we have chosen to focus on work in the free enterprise system—the business world. Within that realm there are many kinds of organizations and jobs that vary in scope and expectations. In looking at different jobs in different settings we make two assumptions: first, that you want to make a decent living, and second, that you want a reasonable degree of job satisfaction. Beyond that there are a range of variables to consider when making decisions about where to interview. This chapter discusses what environments you may pursue, and what you will find in each. We also include suggestions for questions to ask in an interview and guidelines for negotiating the best deal possible once you've decided you want an offered job.

IN SEARCH OF A SILVER PORSCHE

One of the most important decisions you'll make is whether a job and organization match your requirements. Fred worked for one of the large Fortune 500 computer companies. Being considered for a promotion, he was scheduled to be interviewed by a team of vice-presidents. Fred liked his work but always had a nagging feeling about wanting to be his own boss. He decided to take two weeks off before his interview and travel across the country. One day while traveling on Route 80 he passed a couple in a Winnebago with a Porsche in tow. "This man has attained what I strive for," he thought. A few miles down the road he saw the man pull off into a rest area. "A chance to meet my role model," he thought, and pulled off behind him.

Fred approached the man and told him of his situation, the impending promotion, and his reservations. "Don't take it," said the man. "There isn't a day that goes by when I don't look at that Porsche and resent what it cost me." Fred went home, quit his job, and opened a small computer store, where he is his own boss.

If you have been reading this book you're probably not impelled, at least at this point in your life, to quit working for a company and start your own business. We didn't tell you this story to encourage you to do so. What's important about Fred's story is that he based his decision about whether or not he would take the job on what he wanted most from work.

If you're doing a good job at getting interviews and performing well in them, you will get offers that you should turn down. You should turn them down not because they are bad offers but because at this point in your career they are not a good match for you. It is not easy to turn down a job, especially if you are unemployed. But in the long run, waiting for a job that is a good match will serve you better, and will probably lead to a need for fewer interviews in the future. Use as your basis for your decision the extent to which the work, and working for the given organization, excites you. You can avoid much retrenching and maneuvering by not making bad decisions.

QUALITY OF WORK LIFE

One advantage of the diverse U.S. marketplace is that there are choices. Shifting demographics and predicted shortages in many fields mean that for the talented applicant it is a buyer's market. In addition to the kind of company you want, there's a good chance you can choose, to some extent, the kind of work you do. Although most good jobs require a range of focus points, they usually emphasize one aspect of work life more than others. It makes sense to consider jobs that best match your true desires. Your enthusiasm will help you in the interview and lead to more exciting offers.

Mastery

As mentioned earlier, most organizations are seeking people who can perform a broad range of tasks. However, some jobs, by definition, require a mastery of a particular knowledge base or area of expertise. If what you want most in a job is to be responsible for knowing everything there is to know about a particular subject, go for highly specialized jobs. The best way to identify them is by title and specifications. The more specific and detailed the job description, the more likely the company is looking for someone who likes to be immersed in a specific discipline. During an interview, pay attention to the depth and detail of the questioning about a particular subject. This, too, will indicate that the company is looking for someone who can master a given technology.

Exploration

Some jobs demand mastery of known technology, while other jobs are more open-ended. If what you want is opportunity to explore the unknown and discover new ways of operating, go for the exploratory jobs. The best way to identify these is to look for jobs whose descriptions are fairly vague. Employers who are looking for people to uncover new ways of operating often don't have a clear way of describing what it is they are looking for and who it is they want to do it. If in the course of the interview you find the interviewer's descriptions of the duties vague and unclear, you may have found an exploratory job. If the interviewer asks a lot of questions about your ability to tolerate ambiguity and your willingness to work in unstructured situations, you're on the right track.

Protection

If you're someone who cares about quality control, protection jobs may be for you. Protection jobs can take many forms, including auditing, monitoring, observing, even managing. People in protection jobs find themselves occupied with maintaining the quality of products and services by functioning as overseers. The best way to identify such jobs is to look for signs of the organization's concern with your ability to be trusted, your attention to detail, and your sense of rightness or fairness. In hiring for protection jobs interviewers will be particularly careful to ask questions that reveal information about your character.

Caretaking

As companies become increasingly concerned with the human side, one area of growing consideration is motivation. Having employees who know how people tick and can stimulate productivity is critical. If what you like most is to help others develop their full potential, these are the kinds of jobs to go after. Whether you find yourself in a management role or a support role, there are many places in the contemporary organization for the caretaker. The best way to spot such jobs is to look for job descriptions that talk about motivation, productivity, teamwork, and high performance. Employers who are looking to fill jobs with people who can address these concerns are probably trying to fill caretaker jobs. Pay particular attention in interviews for questions about your ability to manage relationships, handle conflict, and deal with difficult people.

Work Styles of the Rich and Famous

Regardless of the type or size of organization you choose to pursue, if you're going for the power positions there are things you should realize. Certain attitudes pervade among those who make it to the top of their field. When Donald Trump, arguably the most entrepreneurial and, to some, most envied man in America, went to the Milton Bradley Company to unveil his new board game, Trump, the Game, his speech to the workers was revealing. Put in overtime, work hard, and you can make it was his message. It's that spirit of commitment of time and effort that you will find those in power expecting of those below them. Listen to his former wife Ivana talk about her supervision of the transformation of the Plaza Hotel and you will realize that neither of these two is lacking in energy toward identified projects. Obviously these

two have tremendous resources at their fingertips. That's not the point.
The point is, even though they could easily sit back and do nothing,
they choose highly ambitious projects to work on, projects that they
have the resources to complete but nonetheless are ambitious enough
so that there is a possibility of failure.

Work, Work, Work

In case you think that either Ivana or Donald Trump are unusual in
their embrace of the traditional work ethic, consider the words of the
leaders of several Fortune 500 companies as reported in the July 3,
1989, issue of *Fortune* magazine:

> I don't think the important traits for good managers have
> changed very much... hard work...
> *Robert O. Anderson, CEO, Atlantic Richfield*

> Too many people today only want to put in a 40 hour week....
> I always told my managers that you can't be successful unless
> you tell your [spouse] not to expect you home for dinner.
> *C. Kemmons Wilson, founder of Holiday Inn*

> The same old qualities are necessary.... You have to be dedi-
> cated.   *John E. Swearingen, Jr., CEO, Standard Oil*

> If I find people who can tell me what's on TV at 8:15 on
> Thursday night, then I'm not interested in hiring them.
> *Rene C. McPherson, former chief executive, Dana Corporation*

> I feel every person can have everything if they are willing to
> work, work, work.   *Estée Lauder*

Whether you agree with these visions of what it takes to be successful in America is irrelevant. If you are interested in securing work
in the better companies you must listen to these leaders. The people
quoted and others like them set the tone for the organizations they run.
If you want to convince those doing the hiring that you are right for

their organization you must approach your intended organization with a sense of zeal akin to these statements.

The Fortune 500

One of your richest options is pursuit of work in the Fortune 500. There are many advantages to working for a big company, as well as some disadvantages. You should think about both before deciding to go ahead. You should also be prepared to respond to your interviewer's inquiries about these factors.

Some advantages of working in the Fortune 500 are:

- The pay and benefits are generally better than those for similar jobs in small companies.
- They tend to have many locations and can give you a choice of where you want to live.
- They often have training programs that can develop your future marketability.
- They can provide an impressive notch on your résumé and open doors to other companies.
- They can often offer other opportunities if you decide to shift into another area.

Some disadvantages of working in the Fortune 500 are:

- Mergers, buyouts, and acquisitions could cause you to lose your position.
- The demands on your time may be more than you want to give. Fortune 500 companies typically expect employees to put in long hours.
- Because of their status, internal competition for the good jobs is often fierce.
- You may be asked to relocate against your will.

Perhaps the most important question you should ask yourself when considering work in the Fortune 500s how central to your life you want your job to be. People who have chosen to work in these highly successful companies revel in their benefits, but it's important to realize the full scope of their commitment. For example, most companies now realize the need to provide adequate support for child care as increasing numbers of women enter and stay in the workforce. You can expect some sort of support, whether in the form of an on-site day-care center or a child care subsidy, but don't make the mistake of thinking that your family's welfare is the company's top priority. No company has made it to the exclusive ranks of the Fortune 500 by placing humanitarian concerns first. This is not a criticism; it is simply a reality. Although many companies have generous benefit packages, their purpose is to lure the most talented, most aggressive workers. Be assured that if you are one of the fortunate applicants to be employed by a Fortune 500 company, you will earn your salary. One of the ways you will earn it is by putting your organization's needs first, even at times at the expense of your family. Being clear about your reasons for wanting to work in the Fortune 500 can make a big difference during the interview, when you're trying to persuade someone that you're a good match. It will also help you ultimately decide whether or not to take the job.

Achievement Motivation

If you are highly motivated, unless you're thinking of starting your own business, the Fortune 500 may be your best primary source of jobs. One of the ways to measure whether the Fortune 500 is right for you is to consider how much you are motivated to achieve. Psychologist David McLelland and his colleagues at Harvard University have spent years studying achievement motivation. Their research shows that some people are more highly motivated to achieve than others. The researchers have devised a variety of simple tests to determine achievement motivation. One test involves a ring-toss game. Participants are asked to play with the goal of winning. They are left to decide, on their own, how they will play. Some people, concerned with not losing, stand as close to the post as possible and get a large number of points. Others, determined to push the limits of possibility, stand as far away as possible, hoping to turn a long shot into a success. The third group takes a middle ground, standing far enough away to be challenged yet close enough to be likely to get a good number of the rings on the post. It is this third group that McLelland would call achievement-motivated. These people, willing to take calculated risks but careful to ensure success, are the type of people likely to thrive in a Fortune 500 environment. It is this kind of success-oriented person that the Fortune 500 companies seek to employ because it is the orientation that matches the companies' commitment to high performance.

Up-and-Coming Companies

If you can't get a job in the Fortune 500 or one of the similarly established companies—or don't want one—other options are available. You may choose to pursue companies that are just getting started or are on their way up. There can be many advantages to such organizations. A company that is hungry for success is more likely to tap the resources of hungry employees, and to a greater extent, than companies that are steeped in tradition. A position in an organization that is creating its traditions can provide an exciting and rich period for your career. You may end up staying in the organization as it matures, or you may take elsewhere what you've learned. Either way, being involved in the growth of an organization will teach you about the ways of the business world. You'll be a more knowledgeable businessperson once you've helped a company to grow, and consequently will be more marketable.

Support Industries

Most people think of the corporate world as primarily offering products and services to the public, but there is another, growing subsector. This growth area offers many fruitful opportunities to potential employees. Many companies, forced to tighten their belts, have chosen to have certain functions performed by outside firms. This has led to an unprecedented growth of support industries, companies whose function is to provide services no longer performed in-house. If your areas of expertise and interest include accounting, human resources, public relations, or a range of other support roles, chances are good of finding work in a firm offering these services. The nice thing about working in one of these organizations is that since their product is support, those who perform support functions are highly valued employees who contribute directly to the bottom line. This is quite different from providing support in-house and being seen as on the periphery of what's really important.

Small Businesses

The small business is by many accounts the wave of the future. According to MIT professor David Birch, smaller firms, companies with fewer than 20 employees, create 98 percent of all new jobs in America. This staggering statistic has many implications for those seeking work. While the figures may be misleading—"new jobs" does not include new openings to fill old jobs—the fact remains that small organizations offer opportunities to those interested in working in them. When you work for a small company you have a better chance of gaining a sense of ownership in the company. Chances are you'll have more of a say in how the organization is run and how it does business. In fact, the small business model is increasingly being recognized as superior to the unwieldy corporate giant, to the extent that even large companies are trying to replicate it by decentralizing their bureaucracies. However, no matter how decentralized a corporation gets, it cannot replicate the dynamism, independence, and entrepreneurial spirit so much a part of the small business. If those are the things that excite you, remember the words of E. F. Schumacher: "Small is beautiful."

Creating a Winning Match

When deciding which companies to interview with, it is important—for the sake of the interview and the subsequent work—that you choose organizations that are a good match for you. We've chosen to focus on interviewing in the free enterprise system—with companies for whom the bottom line is the bottom line. Most of this book can help improve your interviewing performance in the public sector too, but we assume that you are looking for work that provides high earning potential. Many people mistakenly let financial concerns exclusively guide their decisions. As illustrated in the story we told of the Porsche, this sort of blind fortune hunting can backfire. One way to separate your good targets from less attractive ones is to consider what kinds of products and services appeal to you. This is not always as easy as it sounds. For example, you might be drawn to General Electric, whose motto, "We Bring Good Things to Life," might make you believe you will be working for an organization whose primary thrust is providing products to improve the quality of life. You might be surprised to learn, once you started working there, that most of its products are for military use. This might not cause problems for you personally, but it could make a big difference in whether you approach GE and how aggressively you pitch who you are in the interview.

Besides understanding the major emphasis of an organization, you should identify and understand its current thrust. For example, Tom's of Maine is a relatively small company that has created a devoted following by pitching its "all natural" toothpaste to a select group of people interested in natural products. Knowing this, you might present yourself in an interview as someone committed to meeting the consumer needs of this group.

The problem is that Tom's has recently undergone a shift in strategy, is expanding its market, and is trying to appeal to the average consumer. Its product has begun showing up on the shelves in CVS, Stop and Shop, and other major chains. Its marketers are hoping to capture a substantial share of the natural toothpaste market by appealing to the average person, who is increasingly concerned about health.

You might apply for a position in the expanding marketing department of Tom's because you enjoy selling to nontraditional markets. If in the interview you expressed interest by showing your knowledge of the alternative market, you would fall flat on your face. If you really wanted to work with nontraditional markets you would be frustrated working at Tom's today. Tom's is no longer a good match for you.

Beware of the Family Business

Estimates vary, but it is clear that many U.S. companies, large and small, are family-run. Working for a family business when you are not a member of the family is fine, if the top positions are open to outsiders. Nothing is more frustrating to a rising employee than finding the way up blocked by family politics. In many companies family members have been given jobs they can't handle. Consider Wang Laboratories. Wang was such a large enterprise that most observers would not have considered it a family business, but they would have been wrong. In 1986 An Wang, founder of the company, named his son Fred president, although many observers inside and outside the company felt it was a bad move. In 1989, only three years later, Fred Wang was forced to resign, unable, many observers suggested, to follow in his father's footsteps. One can only speculate whether there were other candidates more capable of leading Wang, a company that is now but a shadow of its former self.

Many qualified candidates have lost positions because a family member who was less qualified was given preferential treatment. Nothing is more frustrating than finding your hard-earned promotion short-circuited by the family bloodline. Even though a family business may be a great place to work and you may not find yourself vying for president with members of your company's family, you want to be sure that if the company you are joining is family-owned and -run, there is opportunity for outsiders.

Demands on Time

There was a time, not too long ago, when people talked about working fewer hours, perhaps even with a four-day workweek as the new standard. Like many well-meaning predictions this is one that has not, so far, come true. If you're working in the free enterprise system, whether you're running your own business or working for a multinational corporation, the demands on your time will be great. So great is this demand, reported Suzanne Gordon in an August 20, 1989, article in the *Boston Globe,* that for millions of Americans it has made the workplace a prison. But protesting, reports Gordon, is tantamount to admitting your lack of commitment to the job. The majority of her interviewees demanded anonymity for fear that disclosing these sentiments would hurt their careers.

While there is much talk about balancing work and family, no one in corporate America is advocating less time on the job. In fact some observers of the job market suggest that opportunities for advancement are becoming increasingly available to divorced men and single women, who have less complicated lives to manage than do married people. Although technological advances like fax machines, cellular phones, and e-mail could have resulted in streamlined and efficient work, with less demands on one's time, the opposite has occurred. It's as if someone speeded up the track and all the rats were forced to run faster. On a recent vacation I observed someone faxing material to a home office from a telephone at the beach!

This trend does not bode well for job seekers wanting to preserve their discretionary time, but there are some things the discerning job seeker can do. Some organizations are more demanding than others. Clearly, entrepreneurial companies are more likely to demand long hours than companies that are relatively static (an admitted rarity). While global competition has increased demands to produce more faster, some smaller companies avoid this trap (at least at present). A small business with a distinct market niche may prove less demanding than companies that have competitors lining up at their customers' doors.

Most observers of the U.S. workplace concede that the time crunch is a significant problem. However, in this last decade of the 20th century, when America is facing the greatest global competition in its history, they also concede that things are not likely to get better—at least not for a while. Although there appears to be no way to ensure that your time will be protected, it may be comforting to know you're not alone. More important, if time is really important to you, you may want to seek out organizations that respect an individual's personal time. There aren't many out there, but for those of you for whom it is really important, it might be worth the search.

QUESTIONS TO HELP YOU CHOOSE

There are many questions you can ask your interviewers to help you discover whether the company you're approaching is a good match. Don't ask these questions prematurely, but get answers to them at some time before negotiating the position.

Questions on the Future of the Organization

Knowing what the current leaders of the organization expect in the short and long term can help you decide whether the organization is a good one for you to join.

Possible questions include:

- Where do you see this company five years from now?
- What are the company's long- and short-term goals?
- What is your vision of this company's future?
- What opportunities and threats do you see facing this company soon?
- To what extent has this company met its projected goals?
- What in your opinion is this company's strongest asset for ensuring a prosperous future?

Questions on the Future of the Position

Knowing what part the job you are considering plays in the future of the organization is important. Is the role crucial to the success of the organization, or is it secondary? Understanding the importance of the position can indicate your potential in that organization.

Possible questions include:

- Why was this position created?
- In what ways does the person in this position contribute to the company?
- Under what circumstances, if any, might this position be eliminated?
- Where have the people who have had the position in the past gone from here?

Questions on Expectations

Companies may vary in their expectations from employees. Finding out what a prospective employer expects before accepting a position can save you from surprise, and perhaps disappointment. You may never truly know what a job is like until you're in it, but asking the right questions can give you a tentative view and help you make the right choices.

Possible questions include:

- What would a typical day in this position be like?
- What is the basis on which you judge success in this position?
- What would be the criteria for a raise or promotion in this position?
- What are the standards for rewards, and what are the rewards?

Attitudes About Change, Growth, and Organizational Development

Some companies view themselves as fluid and ever-changing. Other organizations see themselves as stable, secure, and relatively predictable. Depending on your personal and career goals you may want an organization that sees itself one way or the other. While most organizations today cannot avoid change, the quality of work life is different in one that thrives on change versus one that is concerned with staying the course.

Possible questions include:

- What kind of growth do you see for the company in the near future?
- Who do you see as your chief competition?
- What key factors will determine this company's growth?
- In what ways do you think this company and working in it will change in the near future?

POWER NEGOTIATING

The other day I spoke with a woman who had received a call for an informal luncheon interview for a position at a television station. The woman wanted to talk with me about strategies for negotiating salary and benefits. She also wanted to talk about whether or not she really wanted the job and the questions she should ask that would help her to decide.

After a few minutes of listening to all her anxieties about the upcoming meeting I suggested she slow down, relax, and forget about negotiating or whether she wanted the position. Her task for this first meeting, I told her, was to impress the interviewer. If the luncheon ended by leaving the interviewer with the desire to talk to her more, she would have accomplished a great deal.

What this woman didn't realize was that in the negotiation process, timing is everything. The task of the first interview, especially the informal interview, is to get a second interview. The time to think about whether or not you want a position is just before it's about to be offered.

A Small Window of Time

The time to negotiate terms is right after the offer has been made. We like to tell people that during the selection process there is a small window of time during which negotiation is most fruitful. It is during that period that you have the power to negotiate. Before an offer you have no power since there's been no articulation that you are wanted. Once you've accepted the offer, the interviewer has gotten what he or she wants, and does not have to negotiate. Keeping this window in mind will lead to more effective negotiation and greater likelihood of getting what you want.

Preparation for Negotiation

The best way to ruin the negotiation process is not to prepare for it. Many people, caught up in the excitement of the prospect of a new job, assume they can effectively negotiate without preparation. They are making a serious mistake that could cost them thousands of dollars per year. Unless you are clear about what your needs are and the potential for the position, you are at a disadvantage in negotiating. Many people say they can determine their own needs, but finding out the potential for a position is difficult. They are operating under the mistaken assumption that potential salaries are well-guarded secrets.

We know a man who was head of anesthesiology in an area hospital, earning $48,000 a year. He applied for a job in a similar hospital in a nearby state. He got the job and accepted the offer of $55,000 a year. He was thrilled with his victory until he discovered that the posted range for the position was $52,000 to $62,000 a year. His perspective dramatically changed from happiness over a $7,000 gain to disappointment at having accepted a salary at the low end of the range. In his case, a simple phone call to human resources would have given him the range and provided an opportunity to procure an additional $7,000 yearly, thus doubling his increase. When seeking salary information, the first thing to do is to contact human resource to see if the figure is posted. You'll often get a range. If they say the salary range is unavailable your problem is only a little more complicated. The next step involves a little creativity. If you know someone in the organization you may have access to the salary information you need (it's amazing how closely people pay attention to these things). If you have no contacts in the organization and no way you can think of for finding out the salary range, you may need to do a bit of daring investigative work.

Locate a company that is comparable to the one you're approaching. Track down someone in the organization who does similar work to the type you're applying for. Explain your situation and ask if he or she would mind telling you his or her salary, or at least what a reasonable salary would be for someone starting out in that position. You'll find that most people have been in your dilemma and will gladly share the information with you. All you need to do is ask!

Breaking the Price Ice

If possible you should wait for the interviewer to bring up the salary question. Bringing it up prematurely may look improper, and you may have to name a figure before you've had a chance to sell yourself.

Once the interviewer broaches the topic you must decide whether you are ready to negotiate. As mentioned earlier, the negotiating is best left to the time after an offer has been made. If the offer has been made and you feel you have had enough time to represent yourself, enter into negotiation. If the offer has not been clearly made (these things are sometimes unclear) you may respond to the interviewer by asking, "Does this mean you are offering me the job?" If the interviewer says yes, proceed with the negotiation. If the response is no, say something to the effect of "I'm sure we can work something out, but I'd prefer to negotiate once you're prepared to make an offer." This may at first startle the interviewer, but he or she will quickly recognize and respect your need and ability to negotiate from a position of strength. If not, the company is probably not worth working for.

Stacking Your Deck

If you're worth top dollar, and we're assuming you are, one of the ways to get it is to arm yourself for negotiation. To do this identify things about you as an applicant that separate you from the rest of the pool. We recently spoke with a woman who applied for a job in her current organization that was a step up. She was startled during negotiation to be offered $500 more a year than she was presently earning. She knew that the man currently in the position was earning $12,000 more than she was offered (a common problem for women in the marketplace). She asked for a day to consider the offer (a reasonable request), went home, and drew up a list of why she was uniquely qualified for the job and deserved more money. She went in the next day with the list and, by the end of the negotiation, received an offer within $500 of her predecessor's salary. While not every case will have as happy an ending, particularly if you're dealing with discriminatory practices, what's important is the action the woman took. If you're after top dollar, most interviewers want to be persuaded that you're worth it. The best approach is to enter negotiation with a solid rationale for your high salary. A mediocre approach will lead to a mediocre salary. A powerful approach will lead to a formidable salary.

Don't Take It Personally

It's easy to get emotional when negotiating salary, but if you do, you lose significant ground. Remember, negotiation is not a battle but a meeting of the minds. While you have certain needs and salary requirements, the person you're dealing with also has a set of requirements and other people to whom he or she is accountable.

This is not a contest to see who can make the better deal, but an attempt to come to an agreement on a fee for services. This is hard to remember since the process implies a long-term relationship. While your goal is to get top dollar, your method should be a rational presentation of why you're worth it, not an emotional plea of why you want it.

The biggest problem with a personal plea is that it creates an imbalance of power. If the interviewer perceives a sense of weakness in you, he or she may take advantage of your vulnerability. If on the other hand you project a sense of arrogance, you will trigger the other's need to control the situation and you will soon have a battle of egos, a real lose-lose situation.

You probably have more to lose than the interviewer does, but it's important to remember that the interviewer is under pressure too. A successful recruiter, or anyone with hiring responsibility, must develop a good track record for choosing and procuring good people. If you've made it this far, the company is invested in getting you. Don't ruin the opportunity by creating a power struggle.

A Joint Venture

When there's something you really want but are not sure you're going to get, it's hard to see that you are engaged in a cooperative process. At its best the interviewing process is a cooperative venture, the outcome of which will be a joint decision that leaves both parties satisfied. When you think about it, this makes a lot of sense. The ultimate goal for both parties is to create a good match between an individual and a job. The best way to do so is to see and approach the interviewer as an ally, not an opponent. By entering into the relationship with the goal of exploring the possibilities of a potential match, you create conditions that are likely to lead to a successful outcome.

What If There's No One to Work For?

If you engage in an aggressive search process and find there is no one you really want to work for, you have an additional option. You can work for yourself. While self-employment is an attractive option for many people who like the idea of working for themselves, you should only choose it after careful consideration. Self-employment may look attractive, but it is not for everyone. Those who choose self-employment often find they are dependent on others for generating their livelihood. Often, instead of having one boss they now have many, namely, all their customers or clients. When considering whether to pursue self-employment as an alternative to the job hunt, review the following 20 questions. The more times you answer yes, the more likely you will be satisfied and successful. The fewer times, the more likely you're better off continuing on the interview trail rather than the entrepreneurial one.

- Do you have strong planning skills?
- Are you able to shift and adapt your approach when things don't go as planned?
- Do you have the knowledge/skill to run a business?
- Do you have a product/service that distinguishes you in the marketplace?
- Do you have an easy time motivating yourself?
- Does the product or service you have excite you personally?
- Do you have a high tolerance for ambiguity/uncertainty?
- Do you tend to make a good first impression?
- Is there a reasonably good profit margin on your product/service?
- Do you have access to the financial resources to start up a business?
- Do you have an entrepreneurial spirit?
- Do you know of anyone who would buy your service/product?
- Are you willing to give up balance between work and family for the short term?
- Are you willing to work excessively long hours for a while?
- Are you comfortable being a risk taker?
- Do you have strategies for effectively managing high levels of stress?
- Are you willing to have others work for you if necessary?
- Do you have a fallback plan if your business fails?
- Do you have some savings to get you through the startup phase of your business?

- Are you reasonably certain your product/service is as good as or better than the competition's?

While none of these 20 questions by itself is cause for you to choose to start, or not start, a business, each reflects an important consideration when thinking about such a dramatic shift in your relationship to the world of work. Review each question carefully. Spend time focusing on each question you answered "no" and see what you can do to reverse your response. If you find that there are many negatives, you may want to consider staying in the job market and out of self-employment. Many more small business startups fail than succeed, but choosing to work for yourself can be rewarding and satisfying for the right person with the right goods. Make sure, if you choose to take this risk, that it's a smart one for you to take—and one that is likely to lead to success.

POWER PREP STRATEGY VI

This chapter focused on getting a clearer sense of which environments are appropriate for you, given your current needs and interests. On completing this Power Prep Strategy you will have a better idea of which kinds of interviews to pursue and how to indicate that you are a good match.

What kinds of products and/or services really excite you? _____

_____

_____

What size organization do you want to work in? Why? _____

_____

_____

How many, and which hours are you willing to work? _____

_____

_____

How much money do you want? What is the minimum you will accept?

_____

_____

_____

What divisions or departments of an organization most interest you?

_____

_____

_____

This chapter talked about four primary focus points for a person's work (pp. 210–211). What percentage of your time would you like to focus on each? Why? (Your total should equal 100 percent.)

Mastery ____% Reason_____

Exploration ____% Reason_____

Protection ____% Reason_____

Caretaking ____% Reason_____

This chapter discussed four types of free enterprise organizations that you might want to work in (pp. 213–216). Decide how much time you want to spend interviewing in each type, and why. (Your total should equal 100 percent.)

The Fortune 500 ____% Reason _____

Up-and-coming companies ____% Reason _____

Support industries ____% Reason _____

Small businesses ____% Reason _____

You were presented with 18 questions that you might ask, in four categories (pp. 220–221). It is unlikely that you will have the opportunity to ask all 18 questions. Choose one question from each of the four categories that most addresses your needs in this interview.

Question on the future of the organization:

_____

_____

Question on the future of the position:

_____

_____

Question on expectations:

_____

_____

Question on attitudes about change, growth, and organizational development:

_____

_____

Epilogue

By reading *Power Interviews* and completing the six Power Prep Strategies you have prepared yourself to make every interview a winning interview. Careful reading of this book and thorough completion of the activities in it will enable you to deliver a high-performing interview every time. Here is a summary of the key areas you should have mastered:

- Fine-tune the basics of personal presentation.
- Use the inside secrets of interviewing.
- Research the employer.
- Identify and control your personal stressors.
- Understand the needs of the interviewer.
- Demonstrate your mastery of the seven key evaluation factors.
- Refine your answers to the 50 most commonly asked questions.
- Understand and use the key business trends for the 21st century.
- Master your ability to connect with the interviewer.
- Choose a work style that matches your needs.
- Formulate questions to ask in an interview.

Use these points as a checklist for your interview preparation. When you have covered each of the key points thoroughly, you are as prepared as you can be for power interviewing. Go out there, get the interviews, and watch the offers come pouring in!

Index

About the Authors

Neil Yeager is the author of four books published by John Wiley & Sons: *CareerMap*, *The Career Doctor*, *The Leader's Window* (with John Beck), and *Power Interviews* (with Lee Hough).

He is a partner in the Charter Oak Consulting Group, an organization development firm specializing in leadership development, executive coaching, and team building. His areas of expertise include mentoring, leadership, executive career coaching, and organizational change. Current clients include McKinsey & Company, Carrier Corporation, British Petroleum, Otis Elevator and Digital Equipment Corporation.

He is a frequently quoted expert on career and organization development and has been quoted in *Fortune* Magazine, *Money* Magazine, the *New York Times,* the *Wall Street Journal, Inc.* Magazine, and other national periodicals.

For more information call or write:

Neil Yeager
Charter Oak Consulting Group
Mill Crossing Office Park
1224 Mill Street
East Berlin, CT 06023
(413) 367–0194

Lee Hough is the president of The Document Team and founder of the Sales Training Supply Corporation. His companies produce and market programs in sales and sales management. They also produce and market programs in job search, interviewing skills, and assessment tools for hiring and selection.

For information on products contact:

Lee Hough
Sales Training Supply Corporation
9332 North 95th Way, Suite 201
Scottsdale, AZ 85258
(800) 280–1269